How To Sue A Telemarketer

A Manual For Restoring Peace on Earth
One Phone Call At A Time

by Stephen I. Ostrow, Esq.
and
Ozmo Kramer

Illustrated by
Gaspar "Geppy" Vaccaro

How To Sue A Telemarketer
A Manual For Restoring Peace on Earth One Phone Call At A Time
By Stephen I. Ostrow and Ozmo Kramer

AMIGO PRESS
First published in the United States of America, March 2010
Printed in the United States of America

ISBN 978-0-615-33817-0
Library of Congress Control Number 2009913782

BOOK LAYOUT & COVER DESIGN
Michelle Haymoz, Encinitas, www.michellehaymoz.com

CHAPTER & COVER ILLUSTRATIONS
Gaspar "Geppy" Vaccaro

CONTACT & BOOK ORDERS
www.howtosueatelemarketer.com

Dedicated to

the good, kind, and ordinary people of the world

who simply want to have a quiet dinner, or a beer

and watch a basketball game without getting interrupted

by someone who doesn't give a damn about us.

May peace prevail, and may telemarketers see the light

before they pass over, or forever spend eternity

waiting for a straight answer from any of us.

Acknowledgments

It takes a village to raise a child; and a lot of cool people to create a book. I dearly thank my motivational friends Larry Payne and Luigi Sciarra who kept rooting me on towards the finish line when I was stalling. What started out as a leisurely jog in the park turned into marathon training. Too numerous to mention are the friends who laughed at the title "How To Sue A Telemarketer" and by smile encouraged me to continue on.

And to my friend Geppy, who has his own way of saying things, thanks for the illustrations and hard love.

And to my friend Harold Payne, once again, my feet were tired, my mind weary, and my stomach was hungry. And once again, you kept me going and going and going and filled my soul.

There are many ways to say the same thing. Yet without Sheela Alex, Bob DePiano, and Dr. Howard Richmond tweaking my grammar, this book could have rambled on, or worse, got thrown out of court, without their editorial help. *You did good work* mis amigos.

And then there's my buddy Casey who is part of the "do-not-call.com" internet chat group. Research became easy in the busting telemarketers' industry while a part of this group. Everyone was willing to share information on cases and defendants with the common goal of inflicting some pain on these telemarketers. It's always a comforting thought to know we are not alone.

And to Diane and Phil Baum, thank you so much for the final review. I could not think of anyone finer to whom I would share the ultimate in bonding friendship: the pick of Amigo's litter.

I really can't thank anyone for the inspiration of the book. That would be like an author writing an inspirational story on learning to walk again after an auto accident, and then thanking the drunk driver for the opportunity. Perhaps, if along the way, I was able to convince a telemarketer to change his profession, then I would give him thanks and credit for his contribution.

Finally, I want to thank Michelle Haymoz for the kick in the ass down the stretch. The last mile is the toughest and she put the pieces together. Again, I apologize for the arguments on the simple things, but we did have fun! Didn't we?

Table of Contents

"Heads" we kill all the Lawyers,
"Tails" the Telemarketers...

Introduction

The little bastards are at it again. The intrusion by telemarketers has caused ringing all the way to Washington. After some grace of peace and quiet in the home granted by Congress, unwanted commercial telephonic solicitations are erupting again, as if no law was ever passed nor complaints made about this irritating practice.

> "Hello, is Mr. or Mrs. 'I can't even
> pronounce your name right' at home?"

> "Hi, even though you never heard of me
> our records show you wanted me to call."

> "Good evening, last year you told me to
> go to hell and to call you back when
> the Beatles reunited."

Like mosquitoes who have become immune to DDT, the telemarketers are regrouping and brazenly buzzing up the switchboards in search of new consumers' throats to shove their products down. It is not the case of just saying no thank you and ending the unwelcome solicitation; we have a law on the books giving the home consumer the option of whether we want to even hear the pitch in the morning, noon, dinnertime, or night. The telemarketer usually responds to an annoyed consumer's rejection with a pleasant, "You could just politely say *no thanks.*" But that's even more irritating since **we** have the right not to have the commercial conversation in the first place.

When you're talking about prosecuting a flasher, his defensive position is that if you did not want to see me naked, you did not have to look. But luckily, that is not the law. You flash, you crash. It is not whether I want to look or not, but whether I want to prosecute your bare ass.

Sure, there is always a twinge of doubt or guilt about whether we overreact to these minor inconveniences. He's just trying to make a buck. He's probably just coming out of drug rehab. It's better than being homeless. But there's a whole industry out there that is spending millions on soliciting **US** at home, targeting our family time when they scientifically know we will be there (and relaxing). One termite is not a problem. Left unchecked, better call the exterminator.

The unimaginable time is approaching when a telemarketer will call the home because we did not order our regular Thursday night pizza. If we ask for vegetarian, imagine the shock of the order taker if the pattern of pepperoni is broken!

> **"Are you sure you do not want the pepperoni?"**
> **"I said I want the vegetarian!"**
> **"But on Thursdays you always order pepperoni,
> with extra cheese".**
> **"Do you people look thru my window?"**
> **"No, we just keep records."**

Who are these people? Are they just some salesmen trying to make a buck, or a mega economic-social force that offers detailed private information for a premium? Is the intrusive uninvited dinner time call a one time phenomenon? Or can it be an orchestrated scheme designed to track the homeowner's whereabouts and pinpoint our lifestyle and buying habits? Whether deciding on a long distance carrier or mortgage broker, the privacy of one's own home seems to be under attack by sophisticated eavesdropping technicians. Getting upset over one telephone call seems nitpicky; yet combined with those "no one is on the line" clicks iodines the irritation. Is there a connection between the recorded sales pitch and the ghost calls? You betcha!

How the hell do they get away with it? Government must do something about this! Wait, there is too much government! Wait, have you heard about government getting involved with telemarketing and do not call policies? I can't believe my right of privacy can be invaded by them. I can't believe the government can infringe on First Amendment Rights. Where is the balance? Where is the sanity? Where is the fairness? Where is my peace and quiet?

We have a Do-Not-Call law on the books now. The fleas have awoken the sleeping dog. If the telemarketers break the law, they should pay for disturbing our peace. **BUT HOW?** The law gives you the power to irritate the telemarketers in their wallets. That is why you bought this kit. I will lay out for you the step-by-step process of what to do when a telemarketer calls and you want to sue his ass for disturbing your peace.

G.Vaccaro

"Getting upset over
a telephone call seems nitpicky.
One termite is not a problem; left unchecked,
better call the exterminator!"

CHAPTER 1

What To Do
When the Telemarketer Calls

You know it as soon as you pick up the phone. I could name that tune in three notes. As soon as your name is botched or someone is dying to know how you are doing today, it's them. Maybe it's experience, maybe it's sixth sense, but you know it immediately after picking up the receiver. It's not that your brain's computer memory goes through hearing data banks and searches audible wavelengths for that voice. Something about that voice just triggers the alarm, it's them, again.

The victim consumer goes through the usual emotions. The pleasant, "No thank you, you just wasted my cell minutes". The angry, "I told you not to call me when I am making love". The irritated, "This is a bad time, I am boiling my baby and washing my dinner". The sarcastic, "How insensitive to the family, he died yesterday", guilt trip. And of course the annoyed Jerry Seinfeld classic, "Please let me have your home phone number so I can call you back while you are having dinner".

It's no secret, the telemarketer will find you. You can't hide, but we can be ready. If you are reading this manual, you have made the choice to cross over from victim (oh well, what can I do about it) to activist, reclaiming the sounds of silence. Here are some simple "how-to's" in order to commence the revolution. Some may be more obvious than others, but they are all listed here. This manual is for all hair colors.

The most basic tool to combat the telemarketer is information on them. When they first call and give that lame opening pleasantry, telemarketers are attempting to establish rapport. Telemarketers will do anything to engage in conversation, so they will say anything. The telemarketer has a training manual which emphasizes keeping the mark (you) on the line. Keep it going, for the longer the conversation, the higher the chance of a sale. We want to use this to our advantage.

Keep pen and paper near the phone. This sounds so basic, but I cannot tell you how many times I let a S.O.B. off the hook because I had nothing to write with. If you have no definite information on the telemarketer, just chalk it up to another irritation, another hair lost on the way to baldness, another piece of straw on the camel's back. You will not remember the information required below. Start with the basics and write it all down.

Before Mr. Telemarketer can go into his pitch, get him to **repeat** his name, and more importantly, the name of his company. Try to get the information where the company is **located**. The fact that the name and identification of the company is a legal requirement for a telephone solicitation is not something that can be debated at this time. We are undercover. You want to know whether the company is in state or out of state. It will always be easier to collect against a company in state, but don't peter out on out of state violators. The bigger the company, the better.

The longer the telemarketer is kept in the dark that you are writing down information, the less suspicious he will be that you'll be using it for alternative purposes. Get his company's **website.** Remember, his training has taught him to get information on you, not the reverse. He knows he is sneaky. He doesn't suspect that you would want to take action about something he was not profiting from or controlling. We are their marks; we have been charted and diagrammed in their telemarketing courses, not vice versa. Initially, he is intent on establishing a phony friendship, which "friendship" will last the shorter of eternity or getting what he wants.

At this point we must distinguish between sophistication levels of telemarketers. With all due respect, we can tell the high school dropouts reading a script from the ex-carnival racketeers who retired from the road show. Let's address the easy ones first.

The first telemarketer group is made up of rookies and novices who will not deviate from their prepared script. They make us smile because it is so easy to tell how phoney they are and how insincere their presentation is. They do not care about their company or you, simply doing the only job they could get. I don't think they will last in the business; rather they'll be replaced by other irritants who are just looking for work. Nevertheless, the company is liable for breaching our peace when the hired hand breaks the Do-Not-Call boundary.

These people simply do not care. They are at the job for six or eight, or whatever hours they can stand. They read the prepared script over and over. With this group, the idea is not to let them get going on the script. Once the novices are on a roll, they get flustered if interrupted. It is extremely difficult to have a conversation and read at the same time. Everyone has some pride (the one degree of pride out of one hundred is still a degree), and their job is to finish their script.

To be successful at suing a young, unintelligent telemarketer, get the info on them before they go into their schpeel. Do not let them take control of the big rig truck going downhill.

A little scenario after the telemarketer's grand entrance:

"Excuse me, what was your name, again?
And can you spell the name of your company?
Thank you.

And by the way, where is your company located?
Thanks.

Is that where you are calling from?

Do you have a web address?

And one more thing, just in case we get disconnected, what is your telephone number?

Now is that the company's main line, or your private number?

I am waiting for an important call; so if we disconnect, can I call you back?

By the way, how did you get my name?

Oh, I am sure your company has a website, what is it?

Why would I want your company's website?

I just want to make sure you are legitimate. That should not be a problem? Is it?"

Now we are off and running! We have sufficient information to get going. A little research, a little background check, and we are practically off to the courthouse. If you are sitting by a computer, it will seem quite logical that you want to look the company up on the web right away. Of course you have to check out who you are talking with since the telemarketer will be asking such personal questions. With the right inflection, it would be hard for anyone to disagree with the simple request.

I am guessing there is a small part of your revolutionary soul that feels incomplete about the above dialogue. You never got to hit them with the pie in the face about violating the Do-Not-Call law. Once you have all your information, feel free to abuse or vent on the telemarketer in any way that makes you feel better. But remember, the moment you bring up the violation of the Do-Not-Call law, your conversation with this "child of God who has gone astray" is over. Even the dumbest of the dumb will shut off the information valve.

The second group of telemarketers are the polished, slick, and smooth operators. This is not their first "confidence" gig; your money is more important than honesty, decency, or integrity. It's not that they do not know they are breaking the law, it's just simply that they do not care. Unbelievable to me, but they do manage to get a percentage of good people to give them personal information, and yes, sometimes their credit card. Make no mistake; they are good at what they do. As soon as they suspect you are getting data on them, the free informational period is over.

The information required to sue a dumb or slick telemarketer is the same. After all, we want the company, not them. When you get Mr. Smoothy on the line, your sincerity tone must be turned on. These "21st century pirates" are rolling from the time they enter their cubicle until the time it's lights out. Just as you know it's them, they know their market. They have little time for an annoyed consumer. It's a numbers game, and it's "screw you" if you are not playing their game. Even when you know it's them, grit your teeth, put on that smile, and be prepared to get information in a **conversational** way.

Again, the information necessary to file a complaint and achieve a successful outcome is:

1. The name of the telemarketer

2. The company's name

3. The company's website

4. The company's telephone number

5. The company's address

6. What they are trying to sell you

From this information, we can research everything else required to sue the telemarketer. The actual name of the telemarketer is helpful, but not fatally necessary.

As long as you sound interested, the telemarketer will be establishing rapport. Occasionally he will break his rap if rapport is shaken, and some interruption is OK. If they get on their roll, it's ok to interrupt, and ask those pertinent questions. **Do not let him know you are writing down this information.** Our skill is to remain seemingly interested as we collect our necessary data. You have seen the scene in the movies. We are serving coffee to the killer as the cops are on their way. We are keeping the killer talking as the cops trace the phone call. If we can keep the telemarketer on the line answering our few necessary questions, then we can legally punch him out and recoup for the breach of our peace.

The novice litigator will always want to tape the telemarketing conversation. Elliot Ness did it. Hollywood does it. 007 James Bond did it. Perhaps your ex-spouse did it. Hear this one loud and clear. Taping of a telephone conversation **without notice** or permission is illegal in most states. Not only is the taped conversation not admissible in court as evidence, but tables will turn and you will be sitting on the side of the courtroom that says defendant.

There are many ways to deliver notice of taping, but be sure to do it. Once you give notice (even to a pre-recorded message) and get consent, tape away. This will be valid evidence. If you do not give notice and get some type of consent, do not bother attempting to introduce the taping as evidence, even if a dick head telemarketer was on the other end of the line blabbering his unlawful rap.

However, if the telemarketer is flakey enough to leave a solicitation on your answering machine, we can safely say he had notice that he was going to be recorded and it is freely admissible in court. Voice messages are clearly admissible. You can either bring the answering machine into court, or record onto another tape player.

Sony makes a compact digital voice recorder model ICD-P520 which some litigants enjoy. Retail price is around $60. Place it next to your answering machine speaker and have it record the entire tape as you play the messages. The Sony can connect to your computer via USB and transfer to your computer that recording as a single file. Or, just bring in the damn player. Don't be shy about asking a live voice for consent to taping. You don't have to tell him that you intend to sue his ass either.

Try this conversational exchange on for size:

> **"Since we have not met and I am going to buy this product from you, do you mind if I just tape this call? You know, just for my protection.**
>
> **—Why you ask?**
>
> **I am not saying you are, because you seem so nice, but there are other scammers who are out there who are trying to steal my identity.**
>
> **You don't mind if I just protect myself? Thanks.**
>
> **And now what did you want to know?"**

If you get a pre-recorded message, don't feel weird of talking over the pre-record while taping the message. "Please press 1 to connect to live person for more information, press 2 to disconnect". Talk over the stupid taped voice. "I am taping your stupid message which is against the law." "If you do not consent to me taping your illegal and stupid solicitation, you should shut off this machine and never bother me again. If a live person later comes on the line after hitting one of the buttons, it's not your problem, notice was given to his fuckin' machine voice. Seems like they have given some type of consent to me! Once you have given legal notice and gotten consent, the entire conversation can be recorded legally.

Check List Review

- Write it all down
- Name, address, phone, website of telemarketer
- Give notice and get consent if taping

**This blood is sour —
it must have been another damn telemarketer!**

CHAPTER 2

About the Telemarketing Act of 1991 and Updates

Telephone Consumer Protection Act of 1991 (TCPA)

How much litter must people see in the street before their legislature acts to prohibit the dumping of trash? How many stampedes must be witnessed before a politician decides yelling "fire" in a crowded theater should be unlawful? How many bodies must you step over before public intoxication becomes a nuisance? When is enough, enough?

The ceaseless barrage of intrusionary phone calls into the family home climaxed around 1991, when the US Congress finally passed the Telephone Consumer Protection Act of 1991 (hereinafter "TCPA"). The strong public participation on this issue, Congress having heard from thousands of consumers, government agencies and organizations, meant something had to be done about it.

Like all good legislation, the special interest groups lined up on each side. Just because an issue "should be the law", makes common sense, and is supported overwhelmingly by the majority of the common people, it is not an automatic ticket to the law of the land. Competing with the interests of the citizen are the interests of the politicians, and the survival of a politician's political life. For a hungry politician, the hand which holds the most delicious food competes with the plate size of grub.

The most nutritious solution may not be a politician's first choice.

Prosecution for yelling "fire" in a crowded theater competes with the Constitution's First Amendment Right of Free Speech. The government shall not make any unreasonable restraint on the right of free speech. That's an easy argument to overcome since there is no lobby for shouters in a crowded theater. No donations come from the morons who get their yayas from creating chaos.

Prosecution for the unwanted and uninvited bombardment of unsolicited commercial telemarketing into the residential sanctuary also competes with the Constitution's First Amendment Right of Free Speech. The government shall not make any unreasonable restraint on free speech. However, unlike "yelling fire", a lobby exists for the telemarketers of America. A lobby is a group of people or businesses who have similar interests and combine together to pool their money and contacts for the good of their industry. They have a special interest, and are willing to spend to protect their special interest, no matter how unpopular. Politicians like the gourmet green food of lobby groups.

The Telephone Consumer Protection Act of 1991 ("TCPA") passed through Congress, but did not have much teeth. It was a start, but unwanted calls did not stop. The law had as much effect on silencing the conduct of uninvited solicitation as a law prohibiting coyotes from raiding and eating chickens, without the chicken's consent. Restrictions were placed upon automatic dialers and prerecorded voice messages. Unsolicited faxes were addressed. Legal remedies were proposed that were the equivalent of: either having to "sit in time out" or having to say (5) five Hail Marys for repentance. Of course any political donation would take the dog out of the doghouse and allow the installation of more telephone lines for the preservation of capitalism. The Act required the Federal Trade Commission (FTC) to "explore methods" (as opposed to implement methods) to accommodate telephone subscribers from the invasion of unsolicited advertisements, including live voice solicitations. Hmmm, was anybody listening?

The TCPA noted that the privacy rights of the individual and public safety on one hand, and commercial free speech and trade rights on the other, must be balanced by the legislative body. Individual privacy rights had to be protected along with legitimate telemarketing practices. Not bad, if the playing field was level for all players.

Here were the government numbers for the telemarketing industry in 1991:

> $400 billion in commercial activity
> 30,000 businesses employing 300,000 people
> 250 million Americans being bothered
> by telemarketers in their homes

The Government's intent seemed good, and the implementation of the great balance was handed off to the Federal Communications Commission ("FCC"). The government's job was to balance the two interests. Floating around was the suggestion of a National Registry for a Do-Not-Call List. Talk about "a list" had promise, but the mechanics were not clear. Too expensive or too much work for one government agency was the verdict. The idea of a national registry was shelved. "Commercial interests need to be protected!" the lobbyists shouted, and the money flowed and flowed. No unreasonable restraint on commerce balancing with privacy rights was the goal of Congress. The public demanded to cease the noise of pre-recorded and live solicitations. Some exceptions to the prohibitions were carved into the Act. Even with the eventual passage of a national Do-Not-Call Registry, the Act does not prevent all unwanted calls. The balance! Then, and now, the Act does not cover the following:

- calls from organizations with which you've established a business relationship
- calls for which you have given prior written permission and have not expressly revoked
- calls which are not commercial or do not include unsolicited advertisements (we will discuss the commercial creativity later)
- calls by, or on behalf of, tax-exempt non-profit organizations (including political parties and campaigns)

By 1992, the FCC adopted rules implementing the TCPA, but declined to create a national database of telephone subscribers who do not wish to receive calls from telemarketers in general. The FCC opted instead to implement an alternative scheme; one involving *company-specific Do-Not-Call Lists*. The beauty of government! If the consumer did not want to receive any unwanted telemarketing invasions, he just had to sign up with all 30,000 businesses doing telemarketing solicitations. If the consumer really, really wanted peace, some additional effort would be required. Again, the balance. In effect, telemarketers had a free bite at the apple since consumers would not directly complain until an intrusion occurred. Then the telemarketing company for that specific product had the legal obligation to note the consumer's request for non-solicitation.

FCC Rule Making 2003—
The National Do-Not-Call Registry

In 2003, the FTC released an order establishing a National Do-Not-Call Registry and making other changes to its Telemarketing Sales Rules. It seemed that the option of registering with 30,000 companies involved with telemarketing solicitations was not doing the trick that the TCPA intended. Congress approved funding for the FTC's Do-Not-Call Registry as part of the 2003 omnibus budget. The FTC began to take registrations for a Do-Not-Call Registry on July 1, 2003, and the registry went into effect on October 1, 2003. Currently there are approximately 145 million telephone numbers subscribed to the national registry. The celebration of Independence Day remained on July 4th. In the commentary from one of the FTC commissioners:

"By adopting a National Do-Not-Call List, we arm American consumers with a powerful tool to protect their privacy. This is one of the most significant things that the FCC has ever done for American families. It will benefit consumers on a daily basis and in a very personal way. It's certainly the thing that people will notice as much as anything else we have done. We're restoring peace and quiet around the dinner table for everyone who asks for it, and plenty will ask, myself included. The public has sent a resounding directive telling us that uninvited telephone solicitations are not merely a distraction but are driving customers away from their phones. Consumers have also made clear that

our prior rules – without a national Do-Not-Call List – do not work to their satisfaction. And Congress has made its wishes clear by adopting the Do-Not-Call Act which authorized the establishment of the national list. My hope is that our actions here will allow the American public to once again view their phones as a useful connection to the world rather than a source of nightly harassment."

You can now register your residential and cell phone numbers for free, and the numbers will remain on the National Do-Not-Call List forever. Originally enacted for a five year registration, the consumer had the burden of renewing after five years. Remember the green gourmet food? Lobbyists know how to cook. However, recently the rules were amended and the registration is good until you remove your numbers from the list. FCC rules weighed on the side of consumer expectations over special interests. Victory for the common man. Of course, if you desire to remove your name from the national registry, a psychiatric exam will be arranged on your behalf.

Subscribers may register their residential telephone number, including wireless numbers, on the National Do-Not-Call Registry by telephone or by Internet at no cost. Consumers can register online by going to **www.donotcall.gov**. To register by telephone, consumers may call 1-888-382-1222. Hearing impaired number is 1-866-290-4236. You must call from the phone number you wish to register. If you are registering both residential and cell numbers, two calls must be made, each from the respective phone.

Yes, 2003 was a big year in the telemarketing industry. TCPA lost its baby teeth and attained adulthood. The burden of proof was no longer on the consumer, but on the initiator of the call. By registering with the National Registry, the consumer must only show that the registration was in effect greater than the last 30 days. The telemarketing industry now has the burden of reviewing the national lists, and updating those lists monthly to stay current. Consumers do not have to search their records to see if they exempted themselves from that particular violating company. One registration suffices for all telemarketers, and they need to stay current if they choose to remain in the industry. The shift in the burden is a major sign of progress. Failure to do so is an invitation to a lawsuit from astute readers of this book!

Related Rules 2003

In addition to the establishment of a national Do-Not-Call Registry, 2003 contained other amendments to the FTC rules implementing the TCPA. These related rules should either reduce the number of telemarketing calls or give rise to more causes of action:

- If you subscribe to CALLER ID, you should know when a telemarketer is calling you as telemarketers are required to transmit Caller ID information and may not block their numbers.

- Telemarketers must ensure that predictive dialers abandon no more than three percent of all calls placed and answered by a person. A call will be considered "abandoned" if it is not transferred to a live sales agent within two seconds of the recipient's greeting. Hopefully, you are less likely to run to answer the phone only to find silence or the "click" of the calling party disconnecting the line.

- All telephone solicitation calls to your home before 8 am or after 9 pm are prohibited.

- Anyone making a telephone solicitation call to your home must provide his/her name, the name of the entity on whose behalf the call is being made, and a telephone number or address at which you may contact that entity.

In order to verify that your phone number is registered with the National Do-Not-Call Registry, go to **www.donotcall.gov/con-firm/conf.aspx**. It's a good double check to see that our government's systems are functioning. As will be discussed later, not only will you make sure your phone number is on the registry list, you will use the registration as proof at time of trial.

Current TCPA Status

Without a doubt, TCPA has had a substantial impact on the telemarketing industry and the peace and tranquility in the home. There are renegades still out there, and there is plenty of opportunity to bring these bastards to trial. However, the quantity of disturbance is being reduced to consumers' reasonable expectations of privacy. Just as our towns and cities do not have the violence and lawlessness portrayed on the Old West movie sets, crime and violence remain in modern day living. Headlines describing giant settlements in class actions lawsuits by private and attorney general complaints with companies that employ telemarketers for commercial purposes have become more common. Herbalife recently settled their violation for unlawful telephone solicitations for $7 million. DirectTV settled for $3.5 million for unlawful telephone solicitations. More significant, there are smaller judgments against numerous companies in the industry that keep whittling down the unwanted calls. Citations are being written, with fines ranging from thousands to millions of dollars. There is a movement afoot to litigate these violators into compliance.

Headlines describing the loss of telemarketing jobs become more common. Dial America, a telemarketing company with $200 million in sales, has closed numerous boiler-rooms due to cutbacks of telemarketing contracts. According to CareerBuilders.com, faster than you can say job security, telemarketing positions have declined 21% in a telecommunications industry that has steadily grown since 2006. Since the burden of proof has now shifted to the initiators of the telemarketing calls, the ability to use the financial penalties granted under the TCPA allows the public to prosecute and be compensated for violations of their right to peace, quiet, and privacy in their homes. Sad to have a loss of American jobs, but the alternative can be more disturbing. Under the Act, you can either endure the violations, or do something proactive about it. Plainly, it ought not to be cheaper to violate the Act and be sued than to comply with the statutory requirements.

The newest pesky device, the robo calls, automatically generated so telemarketers don't wear out their precious little fingers, is receiving more legislative scrutiny. Several states have narrowed the political exception to telemarketing in the area of the robo calls. If Bill Clinton wants to personally call me and chat about a political candidate, he is permitted to do so under the constitution as free speech. I can live with that. But when

Bill puts his voice on a tape and decides to blast it out to a couple of million people on an auto-generated machine, States have been lumping the political calls with the commercial solicitations and are finding, "the law applies to all autodialer calls, not just consumer transaction calls with commercial messages." More than a dozen states have placed limits or bans on political robo calls, according to Stateline.org, a project of the Pew Center on the States that tracks state legislation. Can you imagine an election where you vote for the issue you want to vote for, and not have to discuss it with a machine on the other end?

The movement is spreading around the globe. Effective September 30, 2008, welcome news afoot for our neighbors to the north who like to dine in peace. As dinnertime telemarketing calls raise the Canadian national blood pressure, help is on the way to quash the annoyance. The Canadian Radio-Television and Telecommunications Commission, which governs telephone, satellite TV, and other communications media, has created a Canadian Do-Not-Call Registry. Violating telemarketers will be subject to a fine of $1,500 for an individual violator, and up to $15,000 for a company violation (Canadian dollars). Registered charities, newspapers, pollsters and political parties will be exempt, along with companies with established relationships with someone at the phone number.

The telemarketers will be required to subscribe to the Canadian Do-Not-Call List and must identify themselves and give a contact number to consumers when asked. Automatic dialing devices that deliver a pre-recorded message will be banned. People can sign up online at **www.LNNTE-DNCL.gc.ca** or by calling toll-free **1-888-866-580-3625 or 1-888-362-5889**.

The annoyance calls will be limited. Charities, surveys, and political crap will not be affected.

Check List Review

- **Residential and personal wireless phone covered by Act**

- **1-888-382-1222 to register with the National Do-Not-Call Registry**

- **www.donotcall.gov to register by internet**

I was so depressed last night that I actually
started talking to a telemarketer from Pakistan.
I told him I was suicidal — he got all excited
and asked me if I knew how to drive a truck.

CHAPTER 3

How To Research the Telemarketer's Legal Name and Address

Sue the bastard, sue the bastard. Kill all the lawyers! Wait, I am my own lawyer. Am I as bad as them? Wait, I didn't do anything wrong. "They violated me".

Should I, or shouldn't I? The dilemma begins. Who will stop "them"? If I want change, I must be the change. My head is spinning, is it worth it? Yes, the decision is made; justice will be done. I will purge the marketplace of the blood sucking, time draining, dark hole of commerce. Now what was their name? Time to commence the research of the **legal** name of the telemarketer and its lair's location.

With the information taken from the original annoying call, first stop on the bus should be the world wide web. Yes, appropriate for black widow spiders. Yes, the research tools are easily available. The ole' search engine can reveal quite a bit. The key when dealing with the court system is to have the correct **legal** name from the beginning.

Sometimes a business will try telemarketing internally. By bypassing the hiring of a telemarketing company, it will usually be a local business performing an unsophisticated operation. The business will not be hiding anything, and oblivious to the law. The local company will use a live voice, and freely disclose all information to you. Duh, this is illegal? The person on the other end will gladly give you everything you need to know. With the publicity of the Do-Not-Call law, this type of disturbance is infrequent and easily squashed once the company understands the law.

In the more common telemarketing cases, there are usually at least two culprits. A company decides to reach potential customers by soliciting over the telephone. Whether the operating company thought of the idea itself, or whether the company was approached by a telemarketing company who sold them on the telemarketing idea does not matter for our purposes. Under the law, both companies are liable for disturbing our peace if they violate the Do-Not-Call laws. Whether illegal pre-recorded messages are used, or violating live voice calls, the two companies are related by agency laws and we want to name both parties as co-defendants. One is good, two is better, and a judgment against both are best.

Sometimes the defendant may be a good old human being, and not a company. Common sense says just use his name. Rarely is it that simple, but it does happen; just spell the name correctly. Sometimes an individual operates under a DBA (doing business as). Not all businesses who operate under DBA's are unscrupulous. However, eventually your legal action will be easier and life more enjoyable if the correct legal name is given from the get-go. There are specific forms that the court uses to join the individual's legal name with his DBA. Don't fight the court's system, if the defendant is an individual doing business as an alias, state the name and the dba (e.g. Bruce Wayne dba Batman).

At the core of the rotten apple telemarketer is legal insulation. A majority of telemarketers will operate as a corporation (INC.) or limited liability company (LLC). The voice on the other end of the phone that has no face attempts to hide its body.

Without ruining this enjoyable manual and creating an overwhelming encyclopedia, corporations and LLC's are basically considered independent people. This legal fiction of creating a new person in the eyes of the law is designed to protect the owner's personal assets in case his business fails. As a broad legislative policy matter, insulation is designed to allow entrepreneurs to take risks in business without jeopardizing everything they own.

If you ever thought about having children so you can protect your assets in their name, skip the difficult labor, the late night feedings, and high cost of the kids' college education; go right to the Secretary of State and organize yourself into a corporation. Without having to take anyone to soccer practice, these "people" can start producing income for you and can legally attempt to hide from the world your identity as the parent of this *bratty child*.

In your search for the correct legal name of the defendant company, as soon as you find an entity that has words incorporated, inc., limited liability company, or LLC after its name, you have probably hit pay dirt. That may be the official name you want as your defendant. Even though its advertisements may not contain the full **legal** name, somewhere on its website or letterhead you may find that info. The full legal name is important. Trust me, these companies that employ telemarketers want you to know that they are either an incorporated or LLC entity.

If Mr. Employer of the telemarketer is hiring this tick to suck your blood, you can be sure this dog has his shots.

I have cleverly recovered from the Rockford Files a second investigative tool. During the original intrusion, the telephone number of the telemarketer was divulged. Even though the coyote called seeking our information, for credibility's sake he must give us some info on his company. Not only for credibility's sake must the telemarketer give us this info, it's the law that a telemarketer must identify himself and not block his telephone number. But as long as the telemarketer is breaking the TCPA by calling a residence, he probably doesn't give a damn about supplying you with the correct and required info. The differentiation between the scam artist who is fraudulently breaking the law and the telemarketer who is just blatantly breaking the law is slight. One is breaking and entering in your front door while the other is just denting the screen door.

Come'on, what the heck, call the number. Usually a receptionist or answering service will answer. She has no clue who you are or what you want. Don't giggle, just give it your best Rockford. If Columbo is more your style, so be it. Ask away. If you feel like getting dressed for the part, any Sherlock outfit will do;

ring, ring...

Hello, U R Broke Oil and Gas Company;
—Is that your official name?

Why do you ask?

—I just want to be sure I am talking with the correct U R Broke.

Yes, we are the original U R Broke, there is no one else like us;

—Is your address 123 Jack the Ripper Lane?

No, we were chased out of there three months ago. We are now located at 666 Devildog Avenue.

—And your website, for more information, please speak slowly?

—Thank you so much for your time, you have been a tremendous help.

Give it your best. Have some fun with them. Be creative. Just get the correct legal name, address, and if you did not get it before, get their website.

Obviously the above investigative steps one and two are the easiest; they can be done from the convenience of your own home or office. Like the movie *Ghostbusters*, if you decide to take on suing telemarketers as a full time profession, more records are available through the State's Secretary of State and the County Recorder's Office. The next chapter will deal more with the Secretary of State when discussing Agent for Service of Process (chapter 4). But for now, the Secretary of State hosts the names of all the legally fictitious children that have surnames of corporation and limited liability company after it. Secretary of State is a state organization, not a federal department. There is one in each state, a total of 50. Once you know the principal place of business, the search for locations is narrowed.

If the directors, officers, and LLC managers are the haberdashers of these fictitious persons, through the Secretary of State we can find which clothes are clean and who is handling the dirty laundry. In these days of rising costs and government bureaucracy, telephone assistance is decreasing and information request fees are rising. Sometimes we must send away for information. Be cool, don't get frustrated, keep searching and the information comes.

The California Secretary of State requires each corporation and LLC to file an annual Domestic Stock Statement. This is true in most states. This form is available to the public upon request made either online or by mail. The same procedure of listing corporate identities is required in each jurisdiction, even if called by different names. This form lists the corporate name, names of directors, officers and agent for service of process (chapter 4). Failure to correct this form yearly can result in the organization falling into bad standing. Bad standing with the Secretary of State can have expensive repercussions for any ongoing business. Again, without turning this manual masterpiece into an encyclopedia, let's say it's in the best interests for any ongoing company to stay current. Ouch, those penalties for failure to comply do hurt. Even if it requires some effort, keep searching; the correct legal names are on file in some governmental agency.

Most states have the County Recorder's Office host the filings of the DBA's. A few states have statewide filings. This is the same office and location where you file those real estate deeds. It may or may not be in the same court building as where your complaint will be filed. Chances are the two county offices are close by, but not necessarily.

When either a person or company files for a DBA, he or it must publish the DBA with a local newspaper as well. Even though the publication is stuck in the back of some magazine that no one ever reads, it's still on a public record in the County Recorder's office.

As previously stated, corporations and LLC's may do business under a fictitious name. This by itself is not a devious act and call to alarm. There can be many valid business reasons for making a DBA other than attempting to cover up and hide the real owners. Remember, not everyone is playing below the corporate radar screen. The procedure for discovery is the same for companies and individuals using DBA's. At the County Recorder's Office you will see the real legal name of the business entity as well as its fictitious name, whether it be an individual, corporation, or LLC. If filing a complaint is necessary against a telemarketer, remember:

> DBA's may be filed by either real people, corporations, or LLC's. Let's say a person named Wanna B. Crooke is doing business as a carpet cleaner. What type of name for a business is Wanna B. Crooke Carpet Cleaning? She files her DBA for Sweet Petunia Cleaning Services. In order for her to get a bank account for Sweet Petunia, the bank will require a DBA which is filed with the County Recorder and published with a local newspaper. By referring either to Wanna B. Crooke or Sweet Petunia Cleaning Services at the County Recorder's reference search, the two names will be cross referenced with correct legal addresses and names.

More and more county recorder information can be found on line and through the web. This is more enjoyable than tramping down to the local County complex; however, sometimes the trip may be a necessary evil. Save gas if possible. Keep It Simple, Stupid (the KISS method) should be your mantra. Do not burn out before you even get into the system. Eventually the names will pop up in the public records if you keep digging.

There are anti-telemarketing organizations out there. Remember, you are not alone. A sophisticated group of telemarketing busters exist on a national basis through a free membership organization. Chances are that a telemarketer on the loose is probably within the sights of this group. If you need a little help from your friends, try joining the site at:

http://www.okiemail.net/mailman/listinfo/prerecord-l

These telemarketer busters are a serious group. Many go at it in small claims court; a few are attorneys who seek out the bigger fish through the superior courts and class action suits. If you are going after a telemarketer, they will be your friend. If you get stuck on a technical question or need help identifying a legal name, they can be a great resource. If you decide to join the big leagues, they can be your allies. The power is in numbers. Once you have signed up and are accepted as a member, then you can post your questions at: **prerecord-1@do-not-call.com.** The most annoying telemarketing calls are the pesky pre-recorded messages. Just as you put the kids down for bed and begin to unwind and relax for the day, the phone rings, and

> **"This is your last chance to get life insurance on your goldfish. Press 1 for more information on how your entire family can be protected from**

dirty tanks syndrome. Press 9 to disconnect and terminate this essential message."

Automatic pilot says to hang up or press 9; get the hell out of here! But wait, you'll never know who keeps calling about them damn goldfish. Take a couple of breaths, be prepared, and press 1. You can experience the emotional rush of the matador upon the releasing of the bull. A live person is about to come on the line. Be cool, play it cool. Get the info on the company. The name, the **legal** name and address. And the website. Get it all. Keep breathing, stay calm, get the info.

This is no time to throw back at the telemarketer that he has the legal obligation to identify himself and his company and give you the information requested. This is no time to inform the telemarketer that if his number is blocked and your caller ID cannot identify him, that is another telemarketer violation. Rather, the years of watching Magnum PI surface to prove that something educational was learned via television.

After getting the necessary info, then let the telemarketer know **to never ever call you again**, please. The use of a pre-recorded message without a prior business relationship is a violation of the TCPA by itself. The fact that you pressed 1 to obtain information to sue does not absolve the telemarketer from liability for the pre-recorded message. Pressing 1 does not mean crap for negating liability, and certainly does not amount to consent for the original phone call. By specifically stating that you do not want any further phone calls, the invitation for future information is negated.

It is hard to believe some of the lengths telemarketer busters will go to get the right name of the company. They are the champions of this extreme sport. They are similar to the outrageous paparazzi when after that celebrity's picture. Putting a charge on a Visa card to get the bottom-line info on a defendant's name and address is the mark of an extreme sport champion. To place a charge on a credit card, get the name and address info as a result thereof, and later fight to remove the charge; it's as heroic as Tom Hanks in *Saving Private Ryan*. It's an NBA all-star performance as opposed to shooting hoops in the backyard. One telemarketer buster put a $300 Visa charge against a health care company, another a $150 Visa charge against a satellite company, and then disputed same for its illegality and then disputed, and then sued for TCPA violations. That's over the top investigation, and certainly worth honorable mention here.

How low will these telemarketers go? Its vicious out there. Besides the annoyance, fraud is included. The elderly are being taken advantage of; bullshit police benefit programs are solicited. You want to go lower? How about telemarketers teaming with unscrupulous attorneys soliciting to do nothing but add their own attorney fees to people already in financial trouble. These are some of the people telemarketing us. Thanks for the call, buddy! Yes, sometime ingenious (devious methods) are necessary to learn who we are dealing with.

We have legislative rights for our peaceful protection. The day that Wanna B. Crooke hires a telemarketer and steps on the flowers of our silent, peaceful garden, a complaint against Wanna B. Crooke dba Sweet Petunia Cleaning Services can be filed. A complaint against the telemarketing company that she hired can be filed as well.

The correct name is very important, and let's get it right from the start. More about this when we discuss Collection of Your Damages in chapter 7.

Check List Review

- Both the company employing the telemarketer and the telemarketer are liable
- Correct legal names are required on a complaint
- DBA's may disguise the true legal name
- State and County agencies will contain the true legal names
- Corporations and LLC's may file DBA's

I was thinking about a career in either
Massage Therapy or Telemarketing.

CHAPTER 4

Agents for Service of Process and Service of Summons

Why, oh tell me why, do I have to go through this process? There are ballgames to watch, laundry to clean, lawns to mow; and here I am having to learn precise rules to sue a telemarketer. My gym membership requires some usage and Fluffy wants to be walked, again. Surely there must be easier ways to stop a telemarketer...

Did I tell you about the contest? Spread the word. If you can come up with a superior mousetrap to stop the telemarketer other than suing his ass, you may win an automatic entry to American Idol's top ten finalists. So far the Federal and State Do-Not- Call Lists have not stopped them. Imagine this, Simon praising the sweet peaceful sounds of silence over the singer who keeps a rockin' tune. You will be a true American hero.

The rules are simple. Stop the telemarketer **without violence.** Any violence perpetrated on a telemarketer will disqualify the entrant. The rules of the Penal Code will prevail. For those who have difficulty thinking outside the box, suggested reading includes *The Butterfly Who Ate Godzilla, My Garden Loves Snails and Slugs,* and *Vacationing in Iraq.* Uniqueness and results of the idea prevail. However, until we come up with a winner, it's back to the courtroom, and good old American justice. Remember the dream, the pinnacle of the mountain climb. You, on Judge Judy, versus the telemarketer.

There is some work necessary before the make-up artist powders your nose for the courtroom cameras. It's not too difficult, but precision helps. As we discussed last chapter, the first step is getting the **legal** name right. Small details, yet there is a world out there which still asks, "What's in a name?" If you check the roll call for this year's graduating kindergarten class, you know what I mean. Just get it right!

After the complaint is filed, eventually it will be *served* on the defendant telemarketer. The Agent For Service of Process basically means a person who can legally receive the complaint with the summons.

You are probably asking right now who can deliver the complaint to the schmuck. **A third person must deliver the complaint to the defendant telemarketer.** It will be quite rare that the telemarketer works right next door to you, but these carpetbaggers certainly can live in your hometown. The plaintiff cannot drive over to the business and personally give to the telemarketer what he deserves. A third person must be used.

If you want a freebie, then it's ok if brother Bob makes the drive across town and delivers the complaint, so long as he is at least 18 years old. After "service" or delivery, a "Proof of Service" form must be filed with the Courthouse where the case was originally filed. Please do not be naïve. If a person can blatantly break the law, don't be shocked to hear in court a defendant lie about whether he received his papers. This could be the same guy that was in his sixth year at community college and still claimed the dog ate his homework. A Proof of Service swears under penalty of perjury the complaint was given to the defendant.

If brother Bob's nickname is Bungle Bob, then perhaps considering a professional process server is a wise decision.

The Sheriff's office provides this service of "service" in most jurisdictions for a fee. It's also helpful to have a sheriff versus a telemarketer when/if the defendant claims he did not receive his papers.

The good news is the joy of imagining a uniformed officer pulling up to the telemarketer's place of business and stepping out of his marked car with the red and blue lights on top, with lots of people rubbernecking as the officer walks into the business to let the defendant telemarketer know your are fighting back.

> "Ah, excuse me, are you _____,
> that a-hole _____ whose been depriving
> the community of telephone quiet time when
> the Senate, House of Representatives, and
> the President of these United States have told
> you to chill out? Well, we will see you in Court.
> Have a nice day."

Oh the exhilaration, the chills running down my back. To feel so good, and without a hangover in the morning. And just wait until our second date.

There are people who call themselves "process servers." They are professionals who deliver legal papers as a full time gig. All lawyers use them. Generally their services are higher fees than the Sheriff (and certainly higher than brother Bob), but process servers can be more useful for the difficult to find defendant. Not all defendants await their legal complaints with open arms. These recalcitrant defendants can give cable tv installers a close run for irresponsibility. Good news about using a Sheriff is that the uniform accompanies the complaint. The bad news is that the uniform doesn't wait around too long. If the defendant is not there when the Sheriff shows, adios amigo.

Hence the need for professional process servers. To catch a thief, you need to think like a thief. To catch a pig, you need to smell like garbage. Not as macho as a bounty hunter, yet excellent pre-school training. Process servers are a better choice when the defendant telemarketer knows you are coming at him and you know his choice will be to avoid you at all costs. Basic companies which are open for business every day at the same location will only require a Sheriff for service of process.

If you hang around a courtroom long enough, you will hear terms such as "personal service" and "substitute service". Personal service is when you give the complaint directly to the defendant. The real flesh and blood breathing mammal accepts the papers from someone on your team. "I give these papers to you, oh sweet child of god." Done, personal service.

Remember those non-breathing paper creation corporations and LLC's? They get served through their officers, managers, or agent for service of process.

Officers are important staff of the corporation who can "bind" the company to legal obligations. General officer titles are president, vp, treasurer, and hot shot secretary (not receptionists), and some higher managers. If you are suing a bank and walk into the bank president's office, you can take it to the bank that is valid service. Since corporations and LLC's work through officers and managers to conduct their day to day affairs, those are who you want to give the docs to.

With that in mind, let me give you your daily dose of realism. These companies through their employees can jerk you around. Government knows this, and so each corporation and

LLC must publish a designee (person or company to accept their service), with the devious title of agent for service of process. Before you ever get into the corporate run around, by checking with the Secretary of State, you can always find the designated agent for service of process. It's a legal necessity. If the Sheriff or process server cannot find someone at the principal office of the defendant, then they can always leave the complaint with the designated agent for service of process. Remember, the Secretary of State will have a listing for every corporation or LLC's Agent for Service of Process.

In the previous chapter, we researched the names and addresses through the Secretary of State. Those same Domestic Stock Statements, or whatever that particular state calls their annual corporate filing, will give the identity of the Agent for Service of Process and its address. Make the most of your fees and use all the information; life is meant to be easy.

If you use a sheriff or process server, they will automatically know to **file the Proof of Service with the Court Clerk.** If you use Brother Bob, Cousin Charley, or anyone else at least 18 years old, it is up to you to make sure the **Proof of Service is filed with the Clerk.** Should I say it again? Maybe not. But I hope you get the picture. If the Proof of Service is not filed with the Court Clerk, then you may have a frustrating morning when your case is called and the judge refuses to hear your case because there is no proof that the defendant had notice. It's a drag to show up in court, wait in court, and go home with a new trial date instead of a judgment. Be sure to **file the Proof of Service with the Clerk Court** well before the court date.

Check List Review

- The complaint must be served upon all defendants

- Correct legal names are required on a complaint

- Person serving the complaint must be at least 18 years old

- Corporations and LLC's are served through their Agents for Service of Process and officers

- Sheriffs and professional process servers are available for hire

- File the Proof of Service *before* the Court date

- Bring an extra copy of the Proof of Service with you to Court

"A telemarketer posing as a doctor
gave a customer six months to live.
Since the customer could not afford the bill,
the telemarketer gave him
another six months."

George must have been flooded
with those telemarketing calls.

CHAPTER 5

Legal Complaints and Forms

Small Claims Court can be a friendly place. Better yet, let's rephrase that with a double negative. A courtroom without lawyers can be a more manageable place; like eating croissants and pastries in Paris where all the waiters speak English. Small Claims is designed to be "user friendly". It's the forum for market place squabbles which replaced the old gunfight at high noon. According to Atticus Finch in *To Kill A Mockingbird,*

> **"There is one way in this country in which all men**
> **are created equal—there is one human institution**
> **that makes a pauper the equal of a Rockefeller,**
> **the stupid man the equal of an Einstein, and**
> **the ignorant man the equal of any college president.**
> **That institution, gentlemen, is the Court."**

Based upon the record number of cases being filed in the court, it is easy to understand why some procedure and organization is necessary in this branch of government.

To just jump in your car without research and attempt to file the paperwork with the county clerk would be like telling a new teenage driver to just go down to DMV and get his driver's license on his birthday. Sorry, life is a bit more complicated than that. To pick up the actual form is a no brainer; GPS your way to the small claims division of your local court or go on line.

However, once you pick up the form, or better yet, before you have form in hand, do your homework!

I'm sure you can convince thousands that your case is the most important matter in the courthouse, but the clerk will not be one of them. If you have followed flawlessly the research in Chpater 3 "How to Research the Telemarketer's Legal Name and Address", you are ready to proceed. If you did not ace the chapter, then its summer school for you and re-read if you want to make your courtroom experience easier. Its amazing, and I mean amazing, how many people you will see at the courthouse having difficulty with names and addresses of the defendants they want to sue. "Is the defendant a corporation? a LLC? a partnership?... duh, don't know?" Better find out, or its to the end of the line. Now you say you have read chapter 3 "How to Research the Telemarketer's Legal Name and Address". Very good, lets move on.

The Small Claims Department is trying to make the system work, but it is facing overwhelming odds just from the sheer volume of the filings. In California as of this printing, the fee is between $30 and $75, depending on the demand for damages, for a plaintiff's filing. The court gives us some bang for our buck. A Small Claim Advisor is provided for free with our filing charges if we are having a problem with any of these questions:

> **Your name, defendant's legal name and address, type of business entity, agent for service of process, why and when the defendant owes you money, if you have tried to settle the case,**

**your zip code, a statement that the telemarketer
is not the government, and number of cases
you have filed in small claims court this year.**

If any other freakin' question comes up from the clerk while trying to get your case filed correctly, the Small Claims Advisor is a welcomed face. Keep smiling. There are not many lines on the form to fill in! Streamlining and simplicity is the intent. Give a summary of the case, the parties involved, why this specific court should hear the case, and how much are you asking for. It can't be that hard, but the failure to *get it right* can be punitive for the unwary. Yes, outright cruel! Yes, get it right. If not, ask the Small Claims Advisor.

All states are different, but let me use California as an example. Small Claims Court has a $7,500 maximum jurisdiction, but a plaintiff can only use the max twice a year. If you attempt to sue defendants more often, then the maximum jurisdiction is only $5,000. I am not trying to make your life complicated; I am merely the messenger. Your state may have different rules, but to rock the telemarketer's boat a jurisdiction of $7,500-$5,000 should be sufficient.

Eventually you will get past the clerk to the big lineup, wherein you will be sitting in the packed courtroom. The bailiff gives the initial roll call. It may be the most heart-thumping part of the small claims system. You may be on the a.m. or p.m. calendar, does not matter, but the bailiff will call all the participants in the courtroom. You look around, looking for a defendant. What does the telemarketer look like? What will he be wearing? Ordinary clothes or a disguise? Perhaps a mask? Perhaps he is there, maybe not? Which one is he, she, or it? The courtroom is packed with 20 other matters; it's crowded inside.

You await the calendar call. The clerk calls out to another plaintiff that there was a defect in his Complaint. A what? What did I do wrong? The legal advisor helped me prepare the Complaint? "Sorry," the clerk says, "she must re-file the Complaint." The clerk moves on. In the next case, the plaintiff has a defective service, and must re-serve the documents. The person protests that the sheriff served the papers, and that should be between the clerk and the sheriff. Clerk says sorry, and moves on. Next case.

There always seem to be something unexpected in life. Some say "shit happens!" Harry S. Truman said, "It doesn't matter how big a ranch ya' own, or how many cows ya' brand, the size of your funeral is still gonna depend on the weather." The drama builds inside the courtroom and your stomach.

You feel the angst of anticipation of having to come back to court. Even some self doubt arises. These returning litigants actually have to come back here, look for a parking place, go through the metal detector, hang out in the hallways, feel their hearts beating with competition drums, and re-present their cases. You are hoping you got it right as the clerk moves down the list to your matter, and calls your case by name. A big lump arises in your throat and your heart begins to beat faster... The moral to the story: read chapter 3 and get it right.

The beauty of small claims is the "simplicity" in the number of forms. Most of the time there is only one document to serve, the Complaint. Sure, it can have a few attachments if there are multiple defendants, or if the complaint is too verbose. This manual is designed to serve the simplicities of life. Sometimes, and only sometimes, a second form or two can sneak in, but we are prepared.

The form will ask at question 3 (in California), "Why are you suing the defendant?" Get your engines gunning, but this is no time to be running on empty. Wow, what a question. I want to bring the telemarketing industry to its knees. Even better, I want to shove the first amendment of the constitution up his phone cord. Oh, oh, oh, I want him to bleed a slow death on the courtroom floor. All quite appropriate answers, but not for this form. Serving the simplicity of life, simply state the following and consider this a gift from the lawyer side of the authors:

Live voice telemarketer (registered with National Do-Not-Call Registry): Defendants violated the Telephone Consumer Protection Act prohibiting the commercial solicitation by telephoning and attempting to sell me (defendants' product) after I registered my name with the National Do-Not-Call Registry on (date).

Live voice telemarketer (not registered with the National Do-Not-Call Registry): Defendants violated the Telephone Consumer Protection Act prohibiting the commercial solicitation by telephoning and attempting to sell me (defendants' product) after I specifically notified defendants on (date) not to solicit me by telephone.

Pre-recorded message (does not matter if registered with DNC Registry): Defendants violated the Telephone Consumer Protection Act prohibiting the use of commercial pre-recorded messages by automatic dialers by telephoning and attempting to sell me (defendants' product) on (date).

Blocked telemarketer telephone number: Defendants violated the Telephone Consumer Protection Act prohibiting the use of blocking the telemarketer's telephone number when

53

making a telephone solicitation after soliciting me on (date) and attempting to sell me (defendants' product).

Failure to Provide Identification by the telemarketer: Defendants violated the Telephone Consumer Protection Act by failing to provide the telemarketer's name, the name of its company, and any way to contact the entity after soliciting me on (date) and attempting to sell me (defendants' product).

Or, if a fax is involved:

Unsolicited faxes (includes residential and commercial phones): Defendants violated the Telephone Consumer Protection Act prohibiting the sending of any commercial unsolicited fax (junk faxes) by anyone unless specifically exempted, by sending me the fax in violation on (date).

I know, I know, you want to make it really precise and have lots to say on the subject, but save that for the trial. Right now, we are serving **notice** on the telemarketing defendant to appear and answer our complaint. **Notice** is all we need to serve, and the details will come later, and so will his alibis and defenses. This is the due process dance, and even the lowest of the food chain deserve to know why they are being summoned to court.

There are conflicting theories on whether we can stack multiple causes of action on the same telemarketing call. The same live or pre-recorded message may come from a blocked phone number, and/or may fail to leave proper identifying information. In more complicated cases, a consumer is allowed to demand to see a telemarketer's Do-Not-Call internal policy manual. Failure to provide the manual to the consumer within 30 days can be a violation in itself. TCPA allows recover of at least $500 for each violation. Is the court willing to grant recovery for each violation stemming from the same solicitation?

An old wise saying is worth repeating, "Pigs get fed, and hogs get slaughtered!" Perhaps stacking two violations in the same complaint is reasonable, three at most. If the judge or commissioner is a telemarketer hater, more fuel for the fire is in order. However, when the asking victim starts to smell like a greedy nitpicker, the credibility of the plaintiff can be affected. We all respect the idealism of a new litigant who hates telemarketers. However, Small Claims Courts are about simplicity and expediency. Most of the time it's better not to distract the court from the primary issue. Remember, asking for treble damages is a part of the TCPA. How many causes of action are too much push? That is your call.

You may subpoena defendant's records as well. A subpoena is a court order directing the defendant to bring certain documents with him to the trial.

Some documents will only be in the possession of the defendant, so it's a fishing expedition on whether the defendant will bring them to court. Don't disencourage, just ask, or demand the documents be brought. For a specific example, see the Addendum. For simplicity sake, request the subpoena when filing your complaint and serve together with the complaint.

The subpoena is optional at Small Claims. It can be helpful, but not fatal, if not issued.

Check List Review

- Determine correct legal name
- Small Claims Advisors are available for assistance
- Fill out Complaint Form completely
- Notice of violation, without too much detail, is required
- Enclose Subpoena if necessary

How To Sue
A Telemarketer

Telemarketing Worksheet

Date:

Time:

Phone No.:

Requested Call Back No.:

Telemarketer Name:

Telemarketer Company:

Address:

Website:

Product:

Telemarketer Manager's Name:

Notes:

That's easy, I used to be a telemarketer
before becoming a banker.

CHAPTER 6

How To Prove Your Case

You, the plaintiff, in a civil court, have the burden of proving your case by a "preponderance of the evidence". What the hell does that mean? In plain English which all levels of education can handle, the scales of justice must tip 51% in the plaintiff's favor.

There are big differences between a civil (small claims included) and a criminal court. The plaintiff prosecutor in the criminal court must score a touchdown to win since certain liberties may be taken away from a defendant. To reap some justice against a telemarketer, we only need to kick a field goal. People were perplexed that O.J. did not spend anytime in jail; yet he was ordered to pay the victims' families multi millions for his killing crime. Its not the law that you can pay X million as a fine for killing your wife. The prosecution only scored a field goal in the criminal trial, and that wasn't good enough to send him to jail. In the civil trial, the evidence was sufficient to award a monetary penalty. That's what we are after, at least a field goal. It does not matter from what yard line, just past the 50/50 scale of justice.

Hold your breath, take a seat, remain calm, and be prepared for the telemarketing defendant to lie in court. That whole raise your hand and put it on the mumo jumbo thing don't mean crap to these people. **Be prepared.** They will show up in court with company telephone records soft toning that their company never called you. Like an old nursery rhyme with a wolf dressed in sheep clothes, with sad puppy dog eyes, they will bring into court either paper or CD company telephone records claiming your phone number is not in their records. **Be prepared,** for most of the telephone solicitations are outsourced. It may come from India, or it may come from the boiler-room down the block, but don't be surprised when their claim of your mistaken identity is proffered.

Your job is to create the images of these boiler-rooms with rows of telephones manned by conning characters. Its not PC (politically correct), but it would be helpful if the judges were reminded of Indian flatbed trucks picking up all English speaking people in the villages for $5 per day and all the curry they can eat in exchange for sitting by these telephones. When these bastards call you, ask yourself, "Where do they get these people?" Try to get the judge to ask himself the same question. Give the judge a hook to hang his opinion on that the records of your telephone call are far far away from his courtroom.

Live voice telemarketer. First, if it's a live voice solicitation, we must show that we are registered with the Do-Not-Call Registry. Yeah, one's personal testimony is legally sufficient, a claim that "I registered with the Do-Not-Call Registry around January XX, 20XX, and that was 30 days prior to defendant telemarketer's solicitation." It's the minimum in evidentiary terms, but not too professional. Courts like to see "hard physical evidence". The simple solution is to go to the Do-Not-Call Registry website at **www.donotcall.gov.** Simply click on *Verify a Registration,* and get written verification of your registration. Simple, clean, and impressive. Your honor, may I introduce Exhibit 1.

If you have never registered with the DNC Registry, then you must show that specific notification was given to defendants informing them of your desire not to be bothered by their phone calls. A specific writing must be produced as your Exhibit 1. Questions will arise as to whether the telemarketer ever received such notice. That is a part of the life of a litigant. If notice went out certified, return receipt requested, no further evidence is required on this point. Make your life easier and do all a favor, register with the Do-Not-Call Registry.

Pre-recorded message. If it's a pre-recorded solicitation, the call is automatically illegal unless it falls into an exemption (charity, political, previous business relationship). Whether or not your name is on the Do-Not-Call List is irrelevant to a pre-recorded telephone solicitation. It is simply not allowed. Testimony and evidence on how you traced the number to the defendant will be most relevant. The evidence of your name on the Do-Not-Call List is dramatic, but not essential. Why not include it? But don't be confused, unless exempt, it's illegal.

Second, a little background is in order. Even though the judge has been barraged by the same harassing calls to give to the blind, orphaned, one-legged dogs who are mentally challenged, remind him of what a pain in the ass it is when the calls keep coming even though you did exactly what the Federal Trade Commission said you must do. Let him know you could have had 10 defendants here, but this was the one you were able to get all the info accurately. Let him know that even though one telemarketer is in the courtroom, that the others got away from your sting. This matter is bigger and meaner than just one phone call, but the time to set example by enforcing the law.

So you say the telemarketer called; the telemarketer says he didn't. Assuming defendant telemarketer produces telephone records evidencing he didn't call, why should the judge believe you? Don't, and I mean don't, produce a tape recorded conversation of the solicitation where it was "all secretly taped" without **NOTICE**. The "ah ha, I got you with a smoking gun" will instantly change into "oh crap, I shot myself in the foot." Secretly recording telephone conversations without notice to the other party is illegal. Even if Alberto Gonzales is your idol, even if you are a staunch supporter of the Patriot Act, even if you have been shopping at Spys R' Us all your life, your world will flip flop. Whatever good you attempted by pursuing a telemarketer will result in you being pursued, you being chastised, you being liable for invasion of privacy. **Notice must be given if you decide to tape a telephone conversation.** Of course this is not applicable if a moron leaves a long winded solicitation on your answering machine.

Chances are that you will be having a relatively short conversation with Mr. Telemarketer once you inform him that the conversation is being taped. If the live voice consents to the taping or just ignores you as he talks over your notice, then your Exhibit 2 is on tape.

If you inform the pre-recorded message that you will be recording the conversation before you "push #1 for more information, or push #2 to disconnect", then that notice should be valid for the rest of the conversation. If a live voice later comes on the phone, your previous notice should be sufficient. It's not your problem that your response to the unlawful pre-recorded message contains your notice of the taping on the call "they" originated.

The much more better approach (if no notice of recording) is giving testimony about the website the telemarketer boasted to you. Chapter 2 discussed the information you need to obtain from the telemarketer. The easiest way to get the defendant's background is by getting their website.

"Your honor, why would the telemarketer tell me about this website if he did not work for this company? I could understand the possibility of mix up in names in a telephone conversation, but not a mix up in websites. The solicitor on the phone spelled out the name of the company and its website one letter at a time. One letter at a time. I took notes slowly and clearly".

Exhibit 3 is the printed copy of their website. "Your honor, I filed this lawsuit after the telemarketer gave me its name and website address."

Even if the defendant company did not have a website, the same reasoning is used for the telephone number given by the telemarketer in response to your chapter 2 inquiry. "Your honor, after picking up the receiver, as soon as I heard the opening come on, I knew right away one of those solicitation invasions was about to occur. I asked the telemarketer to slowly repeat his telephone number just in case we got cut off. I stated I wanted to know something about the company before I divulged rather personal information to this stranger on the other end of the line. He spelled out the name of the company and its telephone number one letter and number at a time. One at a time!"

The ability to remain calm, cool and collected when someone is telling a lie about you is a skill. Trust me, the courtroom will not look like a Jerry Springer show. Decorum will prevail. Plaintiff gets to give his testimony and evidence first. Then the defendant goes. After the defendant presents its fiction, plaintiff gets to rebut. That's legalese for "respond."

A photograph of your telephone display showing the incoming call is great evidence. If you produce a photo of the phone number, the judge will look the defendant squarely in the eye and ask if the phone number is associated with defendant's company. A dramatic point in the trial! Do your investigation ahead of time. If you can't prove the association, then you run the risk of a defendant's lying eyes and fork tongue persuading the judge.

Remember, the person in the courtroom representing the defendant company will not be the telemarketer who actually called you. The voice you heard at the other end of the line will not be present in court. Standing next to you will be a representative who knows nothing about you, but was sent down to the courtroom to deny, deny, and deny. He may know nothing about what happened that annoying day. Rather, he will have a company manual outlining the company's Anti-Do-Not-Call Policy and receipts for purchase of a Do-Not-Call List that the company supposedly purchased to avoid harassing people on the list. He will claim company policy is to check all telephone numbers of all people on the list. He will further claim the company has no record of ever calling you. He will claim a case of mistaken identity. Take a breath. Calm, cool and collected is a virtue.

> **"Your honor, it's too implausible, too unreasonable, too unrealistic to believe that the telemarketer who uninvitedly solicited me is involved with the same business, who spelled out the name, website, and telephone number of this company, which has the same products, and provides the same service as this defendant, can be the basis of mistaken identity."**

Another important point about the Telephone Consumer Protection Act of 1991 ("TCPA") is that the parties not have an existing business relationship. If AT&T is your existing phone company, you are stuck with their solicitations to add onto your phone service; your existing home mortgage company can bug you all they want, **unless you expressly opt out.** However, somewhere in your court presentation, you must state that you have never done business with the defendant company or produce this written opt out notice.

If you claim an oral opt out, be prepared for a nebulous case with an uphill battle. That's not to say it can't be done, but the burden will fall on your shoulders. Be detailed, be exact, and be prepared with names, dates, and circumstances. Do your best, but a written opt out is a stronger case.

I leave the style of presentation of this fact up to your creativity. A simple "I have never done business nor given them permission to call me" is sufficient. If you decide to dress it up... have at it. Judges like creative stories, as long as they are true.

As a side note, "judges" come in all shapes, forms, and sizes. You will find learned statesmen, Judge Judy types, and sometimes you will walk out of court swearing the man in the black robe paid dearly for his position, and many in between. You will find patient judges who understand you are not a licensed attorney, and other judges who feel sorry that the little people in the courtroom are not as smart as them, and many in between. Judges can disagree on the interpretations of the law. Some of the most important cases are decided by a 5 to 4 majority rule by 9 learned Supreme Court justices. It's not that 4 of the Justices are mentally challenged or "got it wrong", but all judges interpret laws differently. When a pitch is on the outside corner, some umps call them strikes, others call it a ball.

I can assure you the Telephone Consumer Protection Act (TCPA) is on your side. Whether the judge interprets the law correctly is determined by elements in and out of your control. Out of your control are the judge's personal prejudices, personal bias, and preconceived notions that he is supposed to keep out of the courtroom. What is in your control is presenting your case efficiently and clearly. By doing your homework, being organized and prepared, and giving supporting evidence accurately will assist you greatly in your case.

Aside from giving articulate and documented facts, be prepared to give the judge "the law". If you find yourself in small claims court for an automobile accident, it's not necessary to define the law. Trust that the judge knows the laws of negligence. However, suing a telemarketer over one phone call can be more challenging to the judge who may be deciding "off the top of his head". Therefore, I suggest supplying the Court with a copy of Points and Authorities on the law.

Does this sound like too much work for this case? You don't feel like spending the weekend in the library? Let me make life sweet and easy for you; see Addendum entitled, "Points and Authorities On Suing a Telemarketer". Since we are dealing with a federal statue, these P&A's are accurate for all 50 states, including Puerto Rico, and can be copied and given to any court... and of course, you are welcomed to use what is in the Addendum. Technically it is not an exhibit, but this is small claims court. Get ready to introduce some additional documentation that the court loves to see and read, "Your Honor, may I present my Points and Authorities as Exhibit 4."

Lastly, before you conclude your case and "the plaintiff rests", some discussion of damages is in order. How the hell does someone figure out how much the pesky telemarketer should pay for disturbing your peace? Good question, that is why it is asked! Small claims jurisdiction in California allows you to ask up to $7,500 in certain cases. Each state is different, but not too far off. The Federal statute allows the States to legislate additional laws pertaining to telemarketers. Commonly, States provide a $500 award against telemarketers, and allow the court to triple the amount to $1500 if the violation is proven to be intentional. That is what is contained in the Federal statutes. Each plaintiff has to check with his own state laws to determine if their state legislature has passed any specific amounts for Do-Not-Call violations. Google is helpful. The TCPA in some instances will allow up to $11,000 for certain violations, but that is mainly for the FCC and FTC (Federal Communication Commission and Federal Trade Commission) regulators. I guess if the right judge got pissed off and the judge brought into the case his own personal experience, you may get the jackpot prize; however, like lotto tickets, a win may be something less than the advertised $50,000,000.

As outlined in your Points and Authorities:

"You are being asked to determine whether or not the law was violated. It is not necessary that you find the plaintiff has any actual injury or actual damages."

Once a violation of the Do-Not-Call Statutes is established, it's up to the Court to determine the amount of the award. Again, courts like help in determining what they should do. Quite common is the use of prior cases or analogous situations. (At the cocktail party, the use of the term "stare decisis" will impress many and gain bonus points). If your state legislators have a specific statute, copy the statute and bring it in. Bringing in an article where the court awarded X in another case is helpful. A written description of damages is looking a lot like Exhibit 5. Each judge is so different; one may treat the violation like a mosquito bite, and another like a gunshot wound. I have a hard time keeping a straight face when I ask for the full $7,500 for the violation, but I can look the judge square in the eye and request $1,500. How are you at poker? Nothing asked, nothing received!

Federal law allows for $500 **per violation**. That amount can legally be trebled, up to $1,500 **per violation,** for willful and intentional violations. There is not much difference in the testimony between the high and low. Basically, it's at a judge's discretion and indiscretion.

A quick review of potential violations:

1. Violation of Do-Not-Call List

2. Pre-recorded messages

3. Failure to identify the solicitor

4. Failure to send the company's Do-Not-Call policy within 30 days after demand

5. Blocking a number when telephone soliciting

Give the judge a visualization. For example, "Voice blasters have claimed in advertisements sending over 1 million messages per day. Five thousand or five hundred dollars is chump change. For fax sender violators, five thousand bucks is 100,000 nickel faxes, and five hundred bucks is only 10,000 nickel faxes." It is all relative.

Once upon a millennium, David Letterman didn't have an agent; he thought he was doing great to be getting a $1 million per year. Later, Letterman wised up and got an agent who negotiated a $15 million per year contract. Even though he had to give his agent more than he was formerly making at $1.5 million, it is all relative. Your average small claims judge doesn't understand the scale of the operation. It's up to you to enlighten him as to the scale of their operation and violations.

Let the court know that you could have had ten defendants in Court today, but this was the one that got caught. Ask the judge to send him back to his telemarketer buddies with a message. You did what the law said you should do when your privacy was violated. Now it's up to the Court to do what the Legislators declared courts should do to these unsolicited invasions. "It ought not to be cheaper to violate the Act and be sued than to comply with the statutory requirements."

Check List Review

- Plaintiff has the burden of proof
- Courts like physical evidence, if available
- Provide documents, websites, and photographs, if available
- Notice must be given for tape recorded conversations
- Expect a telemarketer to lie, and remain calm
- Establish either no previous or expressly terminated business relationship
- Establish no exemption for the telemarketer
- Establish statutory damages
- Provide Court with TCPA Points and Authorities

When asking the court for damages,
impress upon the judge that

*"It ought not to be cheaper to violate
the act and be sued than to comply
with the statutory requirements."*

Just give me your credit card
and I will be sure to send
those delicious cookies to Grandma
with free shipping.

CHAPTER 7

Collection of Your Damages

You went toe to toe with the tiger. Ali and Fraser sparring and dancing in the courtroom arena, each jabbing evidence before the referee in the black robes. For better or worse, no glitzy celebrities like Judge Judy or Jack Nicholson, or television cameras announcing the trial. Good old American justice on a day to day basis, unraveling linens of facts and weaving the facts into blankets of evidence.

The decision comes. Oh my god, the law means what the law says. Judgment for you, the plaintiff! No intrusion means no intrusion. Apologies and denials by the defense are overruled. "This matter is closed. Next case, please," says the Judge.

Obviously, step one of collecting damages is a pat on your own back. Even if you never collect a cent, the satisfaction of knowing you ripped the mask off the monster is a victorious feeling. That voice on the other end of the line insinuating "you can't touch me" has been tagged. The karma of knowing you did something everyone has dreamed of doing deserves a round of drinks at Cheers Bar.

These days, small claim judges do not always announce the verdict from the bench. I know that is not what you see on TV. This can be anti-climatic, and that is exactly what is intended. Judges have no desire of turning their courtrooms into weekday wrestling matches, and chaos is thwarted by announcing decisions by mail. Even if not violent, the after the fact "yes..., but" arguments after verdict by the losers become a drain on court energy and waste precious time.

If a body does show up representing the defendant, try to establish some type of rapport, if possible! Give it a shot. The person may, or may not, have the authority to write a check. I do not advocate "kissing ass", but the chance of a settlement check being written is worth avoiding the added steps of enforcing your judgment. This body may be your contact point in the collection of your damages. Feel him out. If the body does not have any authority or desire to settle, don't waste time discussing politics or human interest stories. Chances are you won't have much in common. But remember, this guy was not the ass who called you; he just works for the company. As an attorney, I have to remind people everyday that I am just the messenger for the *#!&!^ who hired me.

So what happens if the judge awards $1,000, and the defendant will only pay $500 to settle? What should you do if defendant is writing his own rules notwithstanding the amount of the verdict? Welcome to the real world. Let's take a deep breath.

Before answering this dilemma, you have a homework assignment: watch the World Series of Poker on ESPN. After getting the flavor of high stakes poker, you will understand how to deal with your defendant. Depending on the strength of your legal skills versus the defendant's ability to hide its assets, you'll find your answer. I'm not advocating accepting the bird in your hand when you have a net over the bush. No way! However, numerous factors need to be considered before you embark on the arduous journey of collecting money upon a legal judgment.

Factor No. 1: Where is the defendant located? I live in California and have a judgment against a Florida telemarketer for $600. I intend on enforcing the judgment when I visit and see my family in Florida; however, I will not be making any special trips to vacation in Florida just because of the judgment. Be real about it. Convenience has a value when enforcing any legal right! I would certainly consider the offer of a discount on the judgment in exchange for a money order. The magic number comes from the art of negotiation and the strength of plaintiff's position.

Also, our small claim judgments are issued by a State court. Other states will recognize the validity of our judgment; however, there is a court process of obtaining a "sister-state judgment." A little extra paperwork for out of state defendants, a little more of our time taken, a little extra to consider in the enforcement of our judgment. Even though you brought the defendant into your home state for trial, consider whether your defendant's assets are located in your home state. Time has a value. Be smart, for difficult collections have a discounted value.

Factor No. 2: What is the public profile of the defendant? Defendants come in all shapes and sizes. Publicly traded companies on stock exchanges have a more difficult time carrying recorded judgments on their books. A publicly traded defendant is more likely to "pay the freakin' judgment" than avoid collection and publicly disclose the liability on its balance sheets.

The same may not be true for privately held companies. The privately held company who intentionally ignored the Telemarketing Act may intentionally ignore your valid judgment. Thus the collection game of chess is established. Private companies which require a state license to operate their business seem to be easier sources for monetary recovery than those that operate below radar screens. Mortgage lenders, real estate brokers, oil and gas security dealers, chiropractors, mortuary and burial services, general contractors, satellite dishes, banks, and so forth require a state license and maintain a higher public profile. Carpet cleaners, unlicensed painters, unlicensed pool contractors, vacation getaways solicitors, gym memberships, chimney sweepers, and so forth are unlicensed by the state and float around the business community and may require more effort to sink the birdie.

Factor No. 3: How much are you willing to spend on a dead beat? If you have never heard the expression, "throwing good money after bad", learn it now. Doing you own collection work may require a budget. Of course, that requires knowing the amount of the judgment and considering factors 1 and 2.

There is good news and bad news when the defendant does not show up at trial. The good news, getting a default judgment is easier than going through the trial with some lying bastard at the other end of the table. However, if the defendant did not bother to show up at court, there are chances you may be chasing the ghost for quite a while. The cost of the collection must be balanced with the size of the judgment. Each state has its own fee guideline on how much each step of the process will cost.

Recording the Judgment: If you win the case and the defendant will write you a check, the matter is over. If the defendant will haggle and write you a smaller check, see above. If the defendant tells you "to screw yourself", then read on.

Before you hang your judgment up on the wall, record it with the County Recorder. Reminds me of the old Sufi saying, "Praise Allah, but first tie your camel to the post!" The County Recorder is the same place where you record your real estate deeds, which is different from the court clerk who handled your court case filings. You may or may not be in the same county building. This is an important step in collecting your judgment from someone who is not cooperating with you. Through the County Recorder's office the judgment will find its way onto the company's credit rating and public records. Their ability to get a loan is affected. Even if you do not get paid immediately, some time in the future you may receive a call out of the blue by someone needing to clean their credit record by releasing the judgment from around their neck. Hopefully when you get that call, you will be able to put your feet on your desk and negotiate, and gloat, and collect.

Also, if the defendant owns any real estate, the judgment will automatically attach itself to the property in the county. Have you ever heard of a title insurance company? What the hell do they do? Title insurance companies issue insurance or guarantee that a subject property is not burdened by a lien by someone like you who has a judgment against the owner of the property. If someone or a company wants to sell the property, in order for "clear title" to pass, your judgment lien must first be satisfied. So sweet to get one of those calls out of the blue...

Simply, get a certified copy of the judgment from the court clerk, and take it over to the county clerk and ask to have it recorded. The fees should be less than $15 no matter which state jurisdiction you may be in, except for New York, where a cup of coffee costs $15.

The importance of the correct name discussed in chapter 3 becomes evident. We have all heard the horror stories of someone being harassed for having a name similar to someone else. As we look for bank accounts and to lien assets of a debtor, exactness matters. Even though the bastards owe you money, bank and government agencies bend over backwards to protect the right of privacy, no matter how much they owe. It would be a damn pity to come all this way and not be able to collect because of a sloppy name on the complaint.

Executing on Bank Accounts: There are many different ways to collect on a judgment. First of all, I will not thicken this book and describe each and every way to plaintiffs who are just getting started in Small Claims Court 101 litigation. No way, amigos. I would be as uncredible as those shyster telemarketers if I attempted to school you to expertise in this highly complicated arena covered in these 9 chapters. Besides, I will not trade my $150,000 student loan payments for your $15 purchase of this book. I will make your lives easier by laying out what you can do on your own, and what should be handed off to professionals. Executing on a bank account for a small claims judgment is something you should be able to handle.

Before you start the enforcement paperwork, do you know where the defendant banks? If you don't know where the defendant banks, do not start the paperwork on the levying of the bank account. Sounds simple enough. To those who understand, I am not talking to you — to those over-anxious achievers; listen up! Finding out where they bank comes first, then the paperwork to levy on the bank account thereafter.

That's very good advice, Watson, but Sherlock wants to know how to do it. How the hell do you find out where they bank? I have a few suggestions, some more sneaky than the others:

1. Can you pull a legitimate credit report on the defendant? Tricky, tricky area these days of privacy guarded consumer records, but

everyone has different resources at their disposal.

2. Private investigator? Magnum PI had no trouble finding the info. Neither did Barnaby Jones. There is amazing information that company secretaries will reveal these days. Call and ask. Who knows what an employee may reveal? Have fun with your impersonations; test your own creativity. There is a real cash prize for the winner of this creativity contest. Amazing the information that comes your way when one has the "moxy" to ask.

Once you have the bank information you are looking for, then its time to do the bank levy. A bank what? A bank levy is where the judgment is enforced against a bank account. If you have gotten this far and have the bank account info, I know you can figure the rest out with just a little help from your friendly author. We are in this together.

Even if you do not know what a Writ of Execution is, download off the court's website or visit the court clerk and ask for a Writ of Execution form. This writ (form) asks questions that can easily be answered so long as you have a copy of the judgment in front of you. The judgment will not be delivered to the Sheriff or the bank, but the information on the judgment will be transcribed onto the Writ of Execution form. It is your job, not the clerk's, to fill out the Writ. Maybe you can get away with one itty bitty question from the clerk, but do not expect the court clerk to be a full service center. You prepare the paperwork, and then give it back to the clerk. The clerk will then issue the Writ after you pay the court fee. Issue is a fancy legal term for stamping with approval. The fee is not much, $15 in California as of printing, and eventually the defendant will kindly reimburse you via his bank levy. Everyone will want copies of the Writ, so be aware where your local Kinko's copy center is located.

Next you must prepare Levying Instructions to the Marshal, Sheriff, or whomever in your jurisdiction delivers the bank levies. In California we use the Sheriff, but each state has its own officers. This is a question the clerk should be able to answer, "Who delivers the bank levies?" Instructions should be straight to the point. Be prepared to pay another fee to the Sheriff, or whomever, for delivering the levy. This amount is more costly, so again, remember the 3 Factors before laying out the good money.

> **"Please levy on all of the bank accounts of defendant Snidely Whiplash, Inc. at the WeRBroke Bank located at 123 Broadway, Sioux City, CA."**

Unless you can hold your breath for 10-14 days, keep breathing until you get the results. This may be hard to believe, but the sheriff or other officers have other matters besides yours. Once you give up the paperwork to the delivering servers, let it go, get on with your life, and then celebrate when the check comes.

Other Enforcement Techniques: There are a bunch of other ways to enforce judgments; however they require a little more expertise than can be laid out in this chapter. In the words of My Cousin Vinny, "fagettaboutit". For your small claims judgment you do not need to install a Receiver, or Till Tapper, at least not yet. This book is about getting your revenge on the telemarketer, not showing your parents that you completed law school in one weekend.

Remember the three factors. If you ever secure a judgment that is really enormous in size, there are lawyers out there that can assist you post judgment. Lawyers are not allowed to appear in a small claims trial, you must show up yourself. But during collection and enforcement of judgments, you have all your life-lines available. If the time ever comes where you are over your head in procedure, there is a whole industry called "attorneys at law" who can come to your rescue. When someone knows you are suing a telemarketer, people just seem to rally around you.

Once you have a valid judgment, there are companies that are willing to actually buy your victory over the telemarketer. It may not be dollar for dollar, but companies do buy judgments. Included herein are just elementary ways of collecting judgments, but a professional collection company may either pay outright cash or work on contingency for you. This manual is attempting to teach you how to do some simple home repairs, not develop a shopping center. Experience will teach you when to run with the ball yourself, or hand off to a running back.

Check List Review

- Listen carefully to all settlement offers

- Review factors to determine settlement values

- Record the judgment with County Recorder's office

- Determine where Defendant banks before attempting bank levy

- Determine which agency delivers bank levies

How To Sue
A Telemarketer

Spoofin' and Goofin'
on Telemarketers

For belly laughs and the best telemarketing
spoofs and goofs, check out the CD's by
Tom Mabe at www.tommabe.com.

If you do not have at least one belly laugh
listening to Tom turn tables on these
telemarketing leaches, you must return
this book for a full refund and wear
a badge saying "Please help me laugh!"

...you mean if I press number 1,
I will get free tutoring?

CHAPTER 8

Junk Faxes

So these high tech geeks were out on the golf course for their weekend round of golf. As one guy is ready to tee off, there came this high pitch sound, and one of the geeks starts pulling on his ear and talking to himself. An observer queries the strange phenomenon, and is told by someone in the foursome about how the geek was able to install a permanent cell phone in his ear, and he is able to receive the incoming call just by pulling on his ear and talking into a bionic microphone. Remarkable says the observer.

At the next hole, another high pitch sound was heard, and this time the geek hits himself in the stomach, and begins to repeat telephone messages. Again the observer is amazed, and it was explained how an answering machine was permanently ingested and is activated by extreme pressure upon the gastral muscles. Remarkable says the observer.

At the next hole, another high pitch sound was heard, and this time the geek hops over some bushes, unzips his pants, and begins to squat by a tree. The observer just smiles, pokes his buddy, and knows that a fax is coming in...

The issue that is paramount to this chapter is whether or not the fax received was unsolicited or invited. The TCPA is quite clear. Unsolicited faxes are illegal. Unsolicited is a high class name for junk faxes. The days of telemarketers jamming up multitudes of fax machines using speed dialers are over, maybe, or so the legislature envisioned for us. The frustration of losing ink, paper, and time to junk faxes can be transmuted into a viable cause of action against the telemarketer or sender of the fax, and the courts are awaiting the prosecution.

The beauty of causes of action for junk fax violations is that it is so easy. I mean so easy. Telemarketing phone calls require sleuth actions, surreptitious conversation on the phone to collect valuable information, having enough information to prove the case against the unsuspecting telemarketer. Not so with junk faxes; all the info is handed to you on a print at the top of the page or in the body of the fax. Any inconvenience of bringing in the message left on your answering machine is eliminated. No equipment needed at time of trial.

TCPA states no unsolicited faxes shall be sent to any recipient, whether residential or commercial, unless exempted. It does not matter whether the junk fax is sent to your home or office, all is actionable. If you work from home it does not matter whether the phone is registered as residential or work. Unless you have an invited purpose, the sending of a fax without the implied consent is punishable by $500 for unintentional, and up to $1500 for intentional sending of junk faxes.

You may be asking, and I am still asking myself, what is the difference between intentional and unintentional faxes? Anyone who does telemarketing litigation asks the same question. Its like the flagrant foul rule in basketball. There is flagrant foul 1 and flagrant foul 2. FF1 is treated as a technical foul on top of the violation. FF2 you are ejected from the game as a double technical foul. The unintentional violation of the law is when you call the judge "your honor" and he likes you. The violation is only $500. The intentional violation is when you call the judge "you asshole", and the penalty is now $1500. That also means that the judge did not like you. All this is as clear as the skies were at the Beijing Olympics.

"But, but, how can it be so easy?", you may be asking yourself. "Everyone is still receiving junk faxes. How can it remain so prevalent?' It's the same as driving 80 mph on the Californian freeway. Until a patrol car shows up, everyone cruises at their own self imposed speed limit.

Obviously there must be some profit in sending out the junk faxes. The telephone charges versus the profit generated from the responses to the fax seem to warrant the solicitation and violation. It's not until the junk fax sender adds judgment costs to the cost of doing business will there be any changes in the marketplace. As long as there is profit in sending out faxes indiscriminately, the junk faxes will keep coming. The only way the rules will change is by when more and more cases are filed and the man in black (and I don't mean Johnny Cash) hands out judgments for each and every junk fax sent. By suing, you are part of the solution.

In chapter 1, "What To Do When The Telemarketer Calls", we discussed establishing rapport with the telemarketer, conversation with the bastard, paper and pen by the phone to collect necessary data, and getting the telemarketer's website. That was work. But of course, we are trained. Hard work rewards us in the end. We love the stories of how years and years of hard work produce an overnight success story. Boy comes back to the old neighborhood a man, and the home crowd cheers him on.

And, on the other hand, there exists the work ethic of (Bob Denver) Gilligan's predecessor, Maynard G. Krebs, of Dobbie Gillis fame. The first beatnik to appear on national television and probably the most famous beatnik of all time, he liked to sleep until noon. His trademark exclamation, "Work???", guided my youth's philosophy as it does so many today. If you are the type who likes to be right and not work hard, junk fax prosecutions should become your specialty.

You receive a junk fax. Here is the procedure:

Step 1:   Walk over to the fax machine and pick up junk fax

Step 2:   Read the junk fax and determine whether it is a junk fax

Step 3:   Review chapter 3, "How To Research The Telemarketer's Legal Name and Address"

Step 4:   Review chapters 4, 5, and 6

Step 5:   Show up in court

Your case is now ready for submission to the court. How do you prove your case? What do you need to do and have ready? Duh, Exhibit 1 is the fax. Duh, Exhibit 1 has a fax number at the top of the page. If it doesn't, that should be another violation, but that is only being technical. The fax should have a phone number. You have researched the fax number and you know that it belongs to the defendant sender. If not, the phone number on the fax does. Duh, you never had any pre-existing business relationship with the defendant, nor have you authorized any invitation to send the fax. It really is that simple.

Title	How to
Cond	Very Good
User	zbk_list
Station	ZBK09
Date	2023-01-23 11:52:41 (UTC)
Account	ZBK Books
Orig Loc	ZX-2
mSKU	ZBM.LOV1
Seq#	1180
unit_id	7430100
width	0.33 in
rank	1,751,519
Source	YAMSY

delist unit# 7430100

XXXXX

Before you rest your case, take the time to discuss the intentional versus unintentional nature of the action. Perhaps the basketball analogy is **not** your strongest argument. The flagrant foul was good to demonstrate my point, but not yours. Rather, stress that the sending of the junk fax was done for a profit motive. It was done intentionally to make some money notwithstanding the law prohibiting such action. The sender chose to consciously disregard the TCPA in hopes of making a sale. Let the judge know that if you did nothing, if you did not complain, if you did not file this lawsuit, more and more faxes would have been sent out disregarding the TCPA. The defendant sender would have gotten away with something illegal and probably profited from .0001 percent of people who did not complain. The fact that you are in court today evidences an objection to an intentional act which warrants a $1500 damage award under the act. Now you can rest your case.

What type of possible defense can you expect? Because there are more moving parts in a telemarketing violation, there are more defenses. But for junk faxes, there are limited numbers of defenses! You are holding Exhibit 1, their fax with their fax number and business identity on the page. Possible Defenses:

Possible Defense 1:
The fax machine was broken and the number at the top of the fax page is erroneous? The mistaken number is always supported by the body of the fax, the defendant sender's business details. Its such a weak defense, give me a break. Although lying with a straight face can be common in court, this defense would even be too outrageous

for someone who has seen it all. Sometimes your facial expression can be more powerful than words in small claims court.

Possible Defense 2:
A previous existing relationship existed in a past life? Sorry, Charlie, only this lifetime counts. You say you never dealt with defendant. It's up to them to show their invitation to solicit you. The person at trial will only be an employee, without any evidence to show that you had an existing relationship. This defense has been tried and tested, and will not even gain amusement points. Save this puny defense for a new television series, Bombay Law, starring F. Lee Baba Bailey and Harry Krishna.

Possible Defense 3:
I am sorry! Obviously the defendant is stuck by the context of the fax. By saying "I am sorry," may move the violation to a FF1, but will never suffice for exoneration. The goal is win $1500 per fax, but if you walk away with $500, it is a just call for celebration.

There will be people, including those that sit on the judicial bench, who will feel that the punishment is "too harsh" for someone who is competing in the marketplace. Before you allow the court to substitute it's compassion for the law, it is necessary to remind the court that its not the court's problem that a punishment is harsh; it is congress who decides that, and they, in their "wisdom" know best. Instead of me speculating on what the court says, here is the actual language from the leading cases:

"While this particular policy that Congress selected to deter violations may seem harsh to a person or business that has never thought twice about sending marketing materials by fax to its business contacts, it has been long established that harshness (within constitutional limitations) is not a sufficient justification for a court to alter its interpretation of the law. "If the true construction has been followed with harsh consequences, it cannot influence the courts in administering the law. The responsibility for the justice or wisdom of legislation rests with the Congress, and it is the province of the courts to enforce, not to make, the laws." United States v. First Nat'l Bank of Detroit, 234 U.S. 245, 260 (1914); see also Mourning v. Family Publications Service, Inc., 411 U.S. 356, 377 (1973) ("It is not a function of the courts to speculate as to whether the statute is unwise or whether the evils sought to be remedied could better have been regulated in some other manner."); Rittenhouse v. Eisen, 404 F.3d 395, 397 (6th Cir. 2005) ("Although that argument may have merit, it raises a policy question which is properly addressed to Congress, not to the court. '[T]he judiciary's job is to enforce the law Congress enacted, not to write a different one that judges think superior.'") (quoting Bethea v. Adams & Associates, 352 F.3d 1125, 1128 (7th Cir. 2003)).

Make a copy of this quote. In a nutshell, the above is your trial brief when prosecuting junk fax cases.

Check List Review

- Unsolicited faxes are illegal
- Includes both residential and commercial violations
- A previous business relationship is an exemption
- If intentional, ordinary damages of $500 may be trebled to $1,500
- Intentional vs. unintentional is legally confusing

Trial Brief
for Junk Faxes

(see previous page 91)

Why don't we just get back
our old telemarketing jobs?

CHAPTER 9

Specific TCPA Causes of Action

If you were waiting for the sex in the manual, here is the erotic part. It only comes after you have gathered all necessary information from the telemarketer, and you are about to part company. As you grip the phone with your long, tender fingers that have been tapping impatiently, waiting for the super stud to shoot his full load, just tell the telemarketer to "go screw himself" and "shove the phone up his ass."

Too crude for your taste? Or not enough passion? Odds are this is the end of the relationship with the voice on the other end of the line. But if you have sweet talked the Romeo into giving you the necessary data, the love story will continue in court. We don't care so much about the voice on the line, but rather the deeper pocket pimp who hired the voice for the job.

Under the TCPA, each and every violation mandates an individual penalty of $500 against the telemarketer and his team. The legal word of art for compounding the multiple violations from a single telemarketing solicitation is called "stacking violations". Just because the TCPA says so, don't be disappointed if the Judge does not award you the $500 for each and every violation committed during the intrusionary telemarketing call. Even though the authority is given to stack the judgment, judges and commissioners seem to pick out their favorite and award their top one, two or three violations.

Remember, if the defendant telemarketer is a super jerk, the judge can always triple the amount of the violation by labeling it "intentional".

The following are the most common TCPA violations:

I. Violation of the Do-Not-Call Registry
   (47 CFR 64.1200(c)(2)).

The granddaddy of them all. What can be any plainer? I put my name on the damn list, and I don't want you calling me. I know it, Congress knows it, and why can't you just get it, Mr. Telemarketer? As long as a residential phone number is on The List for 30 days prior to the infraction, then the telemarketer is in violation of the Code as long as it does not fall into one of the exceptions (non-profit, political, prior business dealing without revocation). There is a question as to whether the telemarketer is allowed a free "mistaken" call, but most judges ignore that one, too. Hey, one for the good guys. Allege the violation in your complaint succinctly,

> **"Notwithstanding my residence's telephone number was on the National-Do-Not-Call Registry, defendant telemarketer called me attempting to sell me its product in violation of 47 CFR 64.1200(c)(2)."**

II. Violation of Pre-recorded Messages
   (47 USC227(b)(1)(B)

The winner of the 2008 Most Annoying Device. I hate them, you hate them, and judges hate them. When you can finally go behind the pushing of the buttons and find the agent for service of process, what a delight to have his ass in court. His little whine, "You could have just opted out by pushing the 9 button," does not have support in the Code. There is no free bite at this apple; pre-recorded messages without an exemption is just illegal. You play, you pay. Now it's just a matter of how much. If you are able to link the defendant to the call, odds are the judge received the same call. Allege the violation in your complaint succinctly,

> **"Without my consent, defendant initiated a pre-recorded voice message to residence telephone and attempted to sell me its product in violation of 47 USC227(b)(1)(B) ".**

III. Violation of Blocked Name and/or Number
(47 CFR 64.1200(b)(1).

It's bad enough that these bastards are constantly breaking the law, but they are sneaky as well. In our homes we have simple technology, and that enables us to have limited screening of the calls coming in. If the telemarketer broke the law without being sneaky, we would have the choice of whether we want to pick up the call. Do you think there is a reason they would want to avoid detection? When they block their names and numbers, another inconvenience, and another $500 violation. Allege the violation in your complaint succinctly,

> **"Defendant telemarketer blocked it's name and/or phone number in violation of 47 CFR 64.1200(b)(1).**

IV. Violation of Solicitation before 8 AM or after 9 PM
(47 CFR 64.1200(c)(1).

Doesn't your heart just bleed when you get a call in the middle of the night from someone soliciting for the blind and/or dementia? Unfortunately, those calls are not being made by the handicapped, but by telemarketers on commission who don't care a darn about your sleep. When you hear the Asian accents, you understand how they screwed up the time zones. It does not matter whether the telemarketer falls into an exempt category, but even the legitimate charities are not allowed to violate the time rules. If it is not a charity, then stack the violation as well... Alleging the violation in your complaint succinctly,

> **"Defendant telemarketer initiated a telephone solicitation at the hour of ____ in violation of 47 CFR 64.1200(b)(1) prohibiting telephone solicitations prior to 8 am or after 9 pm."**

V. Violation of a Telemarketer to Provide upon Demands its written Do-Not-Call Policy for Maintaining its Do-Not-Call List
(47 CFR 64.1200(d(1)

After the bastard calls you, and you get the necessary info to prepare for the complaint, you unload on the telemarketer and tell him your love story. Telemarketer responds by saying it was an "innocent mistake". After demanding a copy of the telemarketer's Do-Not-Call policy, which **must** specifically outline the company's policy of avoiding these "innocent mistakes", failure to send you the manual is another violation by itself; ka-ching, another $500 violation. Of course it's better to follow up the oral telephone demand with a written demand, but failure to provide the company policy is actionable. Allege the violation in your complaint succinctly,

> **"After oral/written demand, defendant tele-marketer failed to provide me a copy of its written Do-Not-Call Policy Manual for Maintaining its Do-Not-Call List" as required by the Code."**

It's an amazing world. There will always be variety; different strokes for different folks. People will always play it close to the line, and just when the line is established, take another step over. As technology shapes our world, new techniques will be devised to sell us goods. As new violations of the TCPA are invented, new causes of action will be created.

SUPERIOR COURT OF THE STATE OF CALIFORNIA
COUNTY OF SAN DIEGO—CENTRAL DIVISION

HOW TO SUE A TELEMARKETER)

    Plaintiff,)

    v.)   Case No. 2010-123456789

MY COUSIN VINNY)

    Defendant,)

_____)

MY COUSIN VINNY	HOW TO SUE A TELEMARKETER
1. Vinny was a lawyer.	1. No bar exam necessary.
2. Vinny tried his case in a hostile southern town.	2. You try your case in the jurisdiction where your telephone resides.
3. Vinny defended yootes.	3. You defend yourself.
4. Vinny used Marisa Tormei as an expert witness.	4. No expert testimony required. You merely prove the facts of the case.
5. Vinny gets the girl.	5. Getting the girl is up to you.
6. Vinny rubbed the judge the wrong way.	6. The judge hates telemarketers, too.
7. Vinny had to score a touchdown.	7. You only need to kick a field goal.
8. Vinny had to wear a tie and jacket to court.	8. Any decent attire will do in small claims.
9. Vinny would shoot a deer to win his case.	9. No animals get hurt in your matter.
10. Vinny had a thick NY accent and attitude.	10. All you have to do is tell the truth and follow the law.

Telephone Consumer Protection Act (TCPA)

U.S. Code, Title 47, Chapter 5, Subchapter II, Part I § 227.
Restrictions on use of telephone equipment

a) Definitions

As used in this section—

(1) The term "automatic telephone dialing system" means equipment which has the capacity—

(A) to store or produce telephone numbers to be called, using a random or sequential number generator; and

(B) to dial such numbers.

(2) The term "established business relationship", for purposes only of subsection (b)(1)(C)(i) of this section, shall have the meaning given the term in section 64.1200 of title 47, Code of Federal Regulations, as in effect on January 1, 2003, except that—

(A) such term shall include a relationship between a person or entity and a business subscriber subject to the same terms applicable under such section to a relationship between a person or entity and a residential subscriber; and

(B) an established business relationship shall be subject to any time limitation established pursuant to paragraph (2)(G)).[1]

(3) The term "telephone facsimile machine" means equipment which has the capacity

(A) to transcribe text or images, or both, from paper into an electronic signal and to transmit that signal over a regular telephone line, or

(B) to transcribe text or images (or both) from an electronic signal received over a regular telephone line onto paper.

(4) The term "telephone solicitation" means the initiation of a telephone call or message for the purpose of encouraging the purchase or rental of, or investment in, property, goods, or services, which is transmitted to any person, but such term does not include a call or message

(A) to any person with that person's prior express invitation or permission,

(B) to any person with whom the caller has an established business relationship, or

(C) by a tax exempt nonprofit organization.

(5) The term "unsolicited advertisement" means any material advertising the commercial availability or quality of any property, goods, or services which is transmitted to any person without that person's prior express invitation or permission, in writing or otherwise.

(b) Restrictions on use of automated telephone equipment

(1) Prohibitions

It shall be unlawful for any person within the United States, or any person outside the United States if the recipient is within the United States—

(A) to make any call (other than a call made for emergency purposes or made with the prior express consent of the called party) using any automatic telephone dialing system or an artificial or prerecorded voice—

(i) to any emergency telephone line (including any "911" line and any emergency line of a hospital, medical physician or service office, health care facility, poison control center, or fire protection or law enforcement agency);

(ii) to the telephone line of any guest room or patient room of a hospital, health care facility, elderly home, or similar establishment; or

(iii) to any telephone number assigned to a paging service, cellular telephone service, specialized mobile radio service, or other radio common carrier service, or any service for which the called party is charged for the call;

(B) to initiate any telephone call to any residential telephone line using an artificial or prerecorded voice to deliver a message without the prior express consent of the called party, unless the call is initiated for emergency purposes or is exempted by rule or order by the Commission under paragraph (2)(B);

(C) to use any telephone facsimile machine, computer, or other device to send, to a telephone facsimile machine, an unsolicited advertisement, unless—

(i) the unsolicited advertisement is from a sender with an established business relationship with the recipient;

(ii) the sender obtained the number of the telephone facsimile machine through—

(I) the voluntary communication of such number, within the context of such established business relationship, from the recipient of the unsolicited advertisement, or

(II) a directory, advertisement, or site on the Internet to which the recipient voluntarily agreed to make available its facsimile number for public distribution,

except that this clause shall not apply in the case of an unsolicited advertisement that is sent based on an established business relationship with the recipient that was in existence before July 9, 2005, if the sender possessed the facsimile machine number of the recipient before July 9, 2005; and

(iii) the unsolicited advertisement contains a notice meeting the requirements under paragraph (2)(D),

except that the exception under clauses (i) and (ii) shall not apply with respect to an unsolicited advertisement sent to a telephone facsimile machine by a sender to whom a request has been made not to send future unsolicited advertisements to such telephone facsimile machine that complies with the requirements under paragraph (2)(E); or

(D) to use an automatic telephone dialing system in such a way that two or more telephone lines of a multi-line business are engaged simultaneously.

(2) Regulations; exemptions and other provisions

The Commission shall prescribe regulations to implement the requirements of this subsection. In implementing the requirements of this subsection, the Commission—

(A) shall consider prescribing regulations to allow businesses to avoid receiving calls made using an artificial or prerecorded voice to which they have not given their prior express consent;

(B) may, by rule or order, exempt from the requirements of paragraph (1)(B) of this subsection, subject to such conditions as the Commission may prescribe—

(i) calls that are not made for a commercial purpose; and

(ii) such classes or categories of calls made for commercial purposes as the Commission determines—

(I) will not adversely affect the privacy rights that this section is intended to protect; and

(II) do not include the transmission of any unsolicited advertisement;

(C) may, by rule or order, exempt from the requirements of paragraph (1)(A)

(iii) of this subsection calls to a telephone number assigned to a cellular telephone service that are not charged to the called party, subject to such conditions as the Commission may prescribe as necessary in the interest of the privacy rights this section is intended to protect;

(D) shall provide that a notice contained in an unsolicited advertisement complies with the requirements under this subparagraph only if—

(i) the notice is clear and conspicuous and on the first page of the unsolicited advertisement;

(ii) the notice states that the recipient may make a request to the sender of the unsolicited advertisement not to send any future unsolicited advertisements to a telephone facsimile machine or machines and that failure to comply, within the shortest reasonable time, as determined by the Commission, with such a request meeting the requirements under subparagraph (E) is unlawful;

(iii) the notice sets forth the requirements for a request under subparagraph (E);

(iv) the notice includes—

(I) a domestic contact telephone and facsimile machine number for the recipient to transmit such a request to the sender; and

(II) a cost-free mechanism for a recipient to transmit a request pursuant to such notice to the sender of the unsolicited advertisement; the Commission shall by rule require the sender to provide such a mechanism and may, in the discretion of the Commission and subject to such conditions as the Commission may prescribe, exempt certain classes of small business senders, but only if the Commission determines that the costs to such class are unduly burdensome given the revenues generated by such small businesses;

(v) the telephone and facsimile machine numbers and the cost-free mechanism set forth pursuant to clause (iv) permit an individual or business to make such a request at any time on any day of the week; and

(vi) the notice complies with the requirements of subsection (d) of this section;

(E) shall provide, by rule, that a request not to send future unsolicited advertisements to a telephone facsimile machine complies with the requirements under this subparagraph only if—

(i) the request identifies the telephone number or numbers of the telephone facsimile machine or machines to which the request relates;

(ii) the request is made to the telephone or facsimile number of the sender of such an unsolicited advertisement provided pursuant to subparagraph (D)(iv) or by any other method of communication as determined by the Commission; and

(iii) the person making the request has not, subsequent to such request, provided express invitation or permission to the sender, in writing or otherwise, to send such advertisements to such person at such telephone facsimile machine;

(F) may, in the discretion of the Commission and subject to such conditions as the Commission may prescribe, allow professional or trade associations that are tax-exempt nonprofit organizations to send unsolicited advertisements to their members in furtherance of the association's tax-exempt purpose that do not contain the notice required by paragraph (1)(C)(iii), except that the Commission may take action under this subparagraph only—

(i) by regulation issued after public notice and opportunity for public comment; and

(ii) if the Commission determines that such notice required by paragraph (1)

(C)(iii) is not necessary to protect the ability of the members of such associations to stop such associations from sending any future unsolicited advertisements; and

(G)

(i) may, consistent with clause (ii), limit the duration of the existence of an established business relationship, however, before establishing any such limits, the Commission shall—

(I) determine whether the existence of the exception under paragraph (1)(C) relating to an established business relationship has resulted in a significant number of complaints to the Commission regarding the sending of unsolicited advertisements to telephone facsimile machines;

(II) determine whether a significant number of any such complaints involve unsolicited advertisements that were sent on the basis of an established business relationship that was longer in duration than the Commission believes is consistent with the reasonable expectations of consumers;

(III) evaluate the costs to senders of demonstrating the existence of an established business relationship within a specified period of time and the benefits to recipients of establishing a limitation on such established business relationship; and

(IV) determine whether with respect to small businesses, the costs would not be unduly burdensome; and

(ii) may not commence a proceeding to determine whether to limit the duration of the existence of an established business relationship before the expiration of the 3-month period that begins on July 9, 2005.

(3) Private right of action

A person or entity may, if otherwise permitted by the laws or rules of court of a State, bring in an appropriate court of that State—

(A) an action based on a violation of this subsection or the regulations prescribed under this subsection to enjoin such violation,

(B) an action to recover for actual monetary loss from such a violation, or to receive $500 in damages for each such violation, whichever is greater, or

(C) both such actions.

If the court finds that the defendant willfully or knowingly violated this subsection or the regulations prescribed under this subsection, the court may, in its discretion, increase the amount of the award to an amount equal to not more than 3 times the amount available under subparagraph (B) of this paragraph.

(c) Protection of subscriber privacy rights

(1) Rulemaking proceeding required

Within 120 days after December 20, 1991, the Commission shall initiate a rulemaking proceeding concerning the need to protect residential telephone subscribers' privacy rights to avoid receiving telephone solicitations to which they object. The proceeding shall—

(A) compare and evaluate alternative methods and procedures (including the use of electronic databases, telephone network technologies, special directory markings, industry-based or company-specific "do not call" systems, and any other alternatives, individually or in combination) for their effectiveness in protecting such privacy rights, and in terms of their cost and other advantages and disadvantages;

(B) evaluate the categories of public and private entities that would have the capacity to establish and administer such methods and procedures;

(C) consider whether different methods and procedures may apply for local telephone solicitations, such as local telephone solicitations of small businesses or holders of second class mail permits;

(D) consider whether there is a need for additional Commission authority to further restrict telephone solicitations, including those calls exempted under subsection (a)(3) of this section, and, if such a finding is made and supported by the record, propose specific restrictions to the Congress; and

(E) develop proposed regulations to implement the methods and procedures that the Commission determines are most effective and efficient to accomplish the purposes of this section.

(2) Regulations

Not later than 9 months after December 20, 1991, the Commission shall conclude the rulemaking proceeding initiated under paragraph (1) and shall prescribe regulations to implement methods and procedures for protecting the privacy rights described in such paragraph in an efficient, effective, and economic manner and without the imposition of any additional charge to telephone subscribers.

(3) Use of database permitted

The regulations required by paragraph (2) may require the establishment and operation of a single national database to compile a list of telephone numbers of residential subscribers who object to receiving telephone solicitations, and to make that compiled list and parts thereof available for purchase. If the Commission determines to require such a database, such regulations shall—

(A) specify a method by which the Commission will select an entity to administer such database;

(B) require each common carrier providing telephone exchange service, in accordance with regulations prescribed by the Commission, to inform subscribers for telephone exchange service of the opportunity to provide notification, in accordance with regulations established under this paragraph, that such subscriber objects to receiving telephone solicitations;

(C) specify the methods by which each telephone subscriber shall be informed, by the common carrier that provides local exchange service to that subscriber, of (i) the subscriber's right to give or revoke a notification of an objection under subparagraph (A), and (ii) the methods by which such right may be exercised by the subscriber;

(D) specify the methods by which such objections shall be collected and added to the database;

(E) prohibit any residential subscriber from being charged for giving or revoking such notification or for being included in a database compiled under this section;

(F) prohibit any person from making or transmitting a telephone solicitation to the telephone number of any subscriber included in such database;

(G) specify

(i) the methods by which any person desiring to make or transmit telephone solicitations will obtain access to the database, by area code or local exchange prefix, as required to avoid calling the telephone numbers of subscribers included in such database; and

(ii) the costs to be recovered from such persons;

(H) specify the methods for recovering, from persons accessing such database, the costs involved in identifying, collecting, updating, disseminating, and selling, and other activities relating to, the operations of the database that are incurred by the entities carrying out those activities;

(I) specify the frequency with which such database will be updated and specify the method by which such updating will take effect for purposes of compliance with the regulations prescribed under this subsection;

(J) be designed to enable States to use the database mechanism selected by the Commission for purposes of administering or enforcing State law;

(K) prohibit the use of such database for any purpose other than compliance with the requirements of this section and any such State law and specify methods for protection of the privacy rights of persons whose numbers are included in such database; and

(L) require each common carrier providing services to any person for the purpose of making telephone solicitations to notify such person of the requirements of this section and the regulations thereunder.

(4) Considerations required for use of database method

If the Commission determines to require the database mechanism described in paragraph (3), the Commission shall—

(A) in developing procedures for gaining access to the database, consider the different needs of telemarketers conducting business on a national, regional, State, or local level;

(B) develop a fee schedule or price structure for recouping the cost of such database that recognizes such differences and—

(i) reflect the relative costs of providing a national, regional, State, or local list of phone numbers of subscribers who object to receiving telephone solicitations;

(ii) reflect the relative costs of providing such lists on paper or electronic media; and

(iii) not place an unreasonable financial burden on small businesses; and

(C) consider

(i) whether the needs of telemarketers operating on a local basis could be met through special markings of area white pages directories, and

(ii) if such directories are needed as an adjunct to database lists prepared by area code and local exchange prefix.

(5) Private right of action

A person who has received more than one telephone call within any 12-month period by or on behalf of the same entity in violation of the regulations prescribed under this subsection may, if otherwise permitted by the laws or rules of court of a State bring in an appropriate court of that State—

(A) an action based on a violation of the regulations prescribed under this subsection to enjoin such violation,

(B) an action to recover for actual monetary loss from such a violation, or to receive up to $500 in damages for each such violation, whichever is greater, or

(C) both such actions.

It shall be an affirmative defense in any action brought under this paragraph that the defendant has established and implemented, with due care, reasonable practices and procedures to effectively prevent telephone solicitations in violation of the regulations prescribed under this subsection. If the court finds that the defendant willfully or knowingly violated the regulations prescribed under this subsection, the court may, in its discretion, increase the amount of the award to an amount equal to not more than 3 times the amount available under subparagraph (B) of this paragraph.

(6) Relation to subsection (b)

The provisions of this subsection shall not be construed to permit a communication prohibited by subsection (b) of this section.

(d) Technical and procedural standards

(1) Prohibition

It shall be unlawful for any person within the United States—

(A) to initiate any communication using a telephone facsimile machine, or to make any telephone call using any automatic telephone dialing system, that does not comply with the technical and procedural standards prescribed under this subsection, or to use any telephone facsimile machine or automatic telephone dialing system in a manner that does not comply with such standards; or

(B) to use a computer or other electronic device to send any message via a telephone facsimile machine unless such person clearly marks, in a margin at the top or bottom of each transmitted page of the message or on the first page of the transmission, the date and time it is sent and an identification of the business, other entity, or individual sending the message and the telephone number of the sending machine or of such business, other entity, or individual.

(2) Telephone facsimile machines

The Commission shall revise the regulations setting technical and procedural standards for telephone facsimile machines to require that any such machine which is manufactured after one year after December 20, 1991, clearly marks, in a margin at the top or bottom of each transmitted page or on the first page of each transmission, the date and time sent, an identification of the business, other entity, or individual sending the message, and the telephone number of the sending machine or of such business, other entity, or individual.

(3) Artificial or prerecorded voice systems

The Commission shall prescribe technical and procedural standards for systems that are used to transmit any artificial or prerecorded voice message via telephone. Such standards shall require that—

(A) all artificial or prerecorded telephone messages

(i) shall, at the beginning of the message, state clearly the identity of the business, individual, or other entity initiating the call, and

(ii) shall, during or after the message, state clearly the telephone number or address of such business, other entity, or individual; and

(B) any such system will automatically release the called party's line within 5 seconds of the time notification is transmitted to the system that the called party has hung up, to allow the called party's line to be used to make or receive other calls.

(e) Effect on State law

(1) State law not preempted

Except for the standards prescribed under subsection (d) of this section and subject to paragraph (2) of this subsection, nothing in this section or in the regulations prescribed under this section shall preempt any State law that imposes more restrictive intrastate requirements or regulations on, or which prohibits—

(A) the use of telephone facsimile machines or other electronic devices to send unsolicited advertisements;

(B) the use of automatic telephone dialing systems;

(C) the use of artificial or prerecorded voice messages; or

(D) the making of telephone solicitations.

(2) State use of databases

If, pursuant to subsection (c)(3) of this section, the Commission requires the establishment of a single national database of telephone numbers of subscribers who object to receiving telephone solicitations, a State or local authority may not, in its regulation of telephone solicitations, require the use of any database, list, or listing system that does not include the part of such single national database that relates to such State.

(f) Actions by States

(1) Authority of States

Whenever the attorney general of a State, or an official or agency designated by a State, has reason to believe that any person has engaged or is engaging in a pattern or practice of telephone calls or other transmissions to residents of that State in violation of this section or the regulations prescribed under this section, the State may bring a civil action on behalf of its residents to enjoin such calls, an action to recover for actual monetary loss or receive $500 in damages for each violation, or both such actions. If the court finds the defendant willfully or knowingly violated such regulations, the court may, in its discretion, increase the amount of the award to an amount equal to not more than 3 times the amount available under the preceding sentence.

(2) Exclusive jurisdiction of Federal courts

The district courts of the United States, the United States courts of any territory, and the District Court of the United States for the District of Columbia shall have exclusive jurisdiction over all civil actions brought under this subsection. Upon proper application, such courts shall also have jurisdiction to issue writs of mandamus, or orders affording like relief, commanding the defendant to comply with the provisions of this section or regulations prescribed under this section, including the requirement that the defendant take such action as is necessary to remove the danger of such violation. Upon a proper showing, a permanent or temporary injunction or restraining order shall be granted without bond.

(3) Rights of Commission

The State shall serve prior written notice of any such civil action upon the Commission and provide the Commission with a copy of its complaint, except in any case where such prior notice is not feasible, in which case the State shall serve such notice immediately upon instituting such action. The Commission shall have the right

(A) to intervene in the action,

(B) upon so intervening, to be heard on all matters arising therein, and

(C) to file petitions for appeal.

(4) Venue; service of process

Any civil action brought under this subsection in a district court of the United States may be brought in the district wherein the defendant is found or is an inhabitant or transacts business or wherein the violation occurred or is occurring, and process in such cases may be served in any district in which the defendant is an inhabitant or where the defendant may be found.

(5) Investigatory powers

For purposes of bringing any civil action under this subsection, nothing in this section shall prevent the attorney general of a State, or an official or agency designated by a State, from exercising the powers conferred on the attorney general or such official by the laws of such State to conduct investigations or to administer oaths or affirmations or to compel the attendance of witnesses or the production of documentary and other evidence.

(6) Effect on State court proceedings

Nothing contained in this subsection shall be construed to prohibit an authorized State official from proceeding in State court on the basis of an alleged violation of any general civil or criminal statute of such State.

(7) Limitation

Whenever the Commission has instituted a civil action for violation of regulations prescribed under this section, no State may, during the pendency of such action instituted by the Commission, subsequently institute a civil action against any defendant named in the Commission's complaint for any violation as alleged in the Commission's complaint.

(8) "Attorney general" defined

As used in this subsection, the term "attorney general" means the chief legal officer of a State.

(g) Junk fax enforcement report

The Commission shall submit an annual report to Congress regarding the enforcement during the past year of the provisions of this section relating to sending of unsolicited advertisements to telephone facsimile machines, which report shall include—

(1) the number of complaints received by the Commission during such year alleging that a consumer received an unsolicited advertisement via telephone facsimile machine in violation of the Commission's rules;

(2) the number of citations issued by the Commission pursuant to section 503 of this title during the year to enforce any law, regulation, or policy relating to sending of unsolicited advertisements to telephone facsimile machines;

(3) the number of notices of apparent liability issued by the Commission pursuant to section 503 of this title during the year to enforce any law, regulation,

or policy relating to sending of unsolicited advertisements to telephone facsimile machines;

(4) for each notice referred to in paragraph (3)—

(A) the amount of the proposed forfeiture penalty involved;

(B) the person to whom the notice was issued;

(C) the length of time between the date on which the complaint was filed and the date on which the notice was issued; and

(D) the status of the proceeding;

(5) the number of final orders imposing forfeiture penalties issued pursuant to section 503 of this title during the year to enforce any law, regulation, or policy relating to sending of unsolicited advertisements to telephone facsimile machines;

(6) for each forfeiture order referred to in paragraph (5)—

(A) the amount of the penalty imposed by the order;

(B) the person to whom the order was issued;

(C) whether the forfeiture penalty has been paid; and

(D) the amount paid;

(7) for each case in which a person has failed to pay a forfeiture penalty imposed by such a final order, whether the Commission referred such matter for recovery of the penalty; and

(8) for each case in which the Commission referred such an order for recovery—

(A) the number of days from the date the Commission issued such order to the date of such referral;

(B) whether an action has been commenced to recover the penalty, and if so, the number of days from the date the Commission referred such order for recovery to the date of such commencement; and

(C) whether the recovery action resulted in collection of any amount, and if so, the amount collected.

Federal Communications Commission

Note: CFR § 64.1200 was enacted as a result of the Telephone Consumer Protection Act (TCPA). The TCPA offers consumers a "Private Right Of Action" for violating "the regulations prescribed under this subsection". The regulations below are the regulations referenced by the TCPA.

47 CFR §64.1200 Subpart L--Restrictions on Telephone Solicitation

§64.1200 Delivery restrictions.

[Code of Federal Regulations]

[Title 47, Volume 3]

[Revised as of October 1, 2004]

TITLE 47--TELECOMMUNICATION

CHAPTER I--FEDERAL COMMUNICATIONS COMMISSION

PART 64_MISCELLANEOUS RULES RELATING TO COMMON CARRIERS

Subpart L_Restrictions on Telemarketing and Telephone Solicitation

Sec. 64.1200 Delivery restrictions.

(a) No person or entity may:

(1) Initiate any telephone call (other than a call made for emergency purposes or made with the prior express consent of the called

party) using an automatic telephone dialing system or an artificial or prerecorded voice,

(i) To any emergency telephone line, including any 911 line and any emergency line of a hospital, medical physician or service office,

health care facility, poison control center, or fire protection or law enforcement agency;

(ii) To the telephone line of any guest room or patient room of a hospital, health care facility, elderly home, or similar establishment; or

(iii) To any telephone number assigned to a paging service, cellular telephone service, specialized mobile radio service, or other radio common carrier service, or any service for which the called party is charged for the call.

(2) Initiate any telephone call to any residential line using an artificial or pre-recorded voice to deliver a message without the prior express consent of the called party, unless the call,

(i) Is made for emergency purposes,

(ii) Is not made for a commercial purpose,

(iii) Is made for a commercial purpose but does not include or introduce an unsolicited advertisement or constitute a telephone solicitation,

(iv) Is made to any person with whom the caller has an established business relationship at the time the call is made, or

(v) Is made by or on behalf of a tax-exempt nonprofit organization.

(3) Use a telephone facsimile machine, computer, or other device to send an unsolicited advertisement to a telephone facsimile machine,

(i) For purposes of paragraph (a)(3) of this section, a facsimile advertisement is not ``unsolicited'' if the recipient has granted the sender prior express invitation or permission to deliver the advertisement, as evidenced by a signed, written statement that includes the facsimile number to which any advertisements may be sent and clearly indicates the recipient's consent to receive such facsimile advertisements from the sender.

(ii) A facsimile broadcaster will be liable for violations of paragraph (a)(3) of this section if it demonstrates a high degree of involvement in, or actual notice of, the unlawful activity and fails to take steps to prevent such facsimile transmissions.

(4) Use an automatic telephone dialing system in such a way that two or more telephone lines of a multi-line business are engaged simultaneously.

(5) Disconnect an unanswered telemarketing call prior to at least 15 seconds or four (4) rings.

(6) Abandon more than three percent of all telemarketing calls that are answered live by a person, measured over a 30-day period. A call is "abandoned" if it is not connected to a live sales representative within two (2) seconds of the called person's completed greeting.

Whenever a sales representative is not available to speak with the person answering the call, that person must receive, within two (2) seconds after the called person's completed greeting, a prerecorded identification message that states only the name and telephone number of the business, entity, or individual on whose behalf the call was placed, and that the call was for ``telemarketing purposes.'' The telephone number so provided must permit any individual to make a do-not-call request during regular business hours for the duration of the telemarketing campaign. The telephone number may not be a 900 number or any other number for which charges exceed local or long distance transmission charges. The seller or telemarketer must maintain records establishing compliance with paragraph (a)(6) of this section.

(i) A call for telemarketing purposes that delivers an artificial or prerecorded voice message to a residential telephone line that is assigned to a person who either has granted prior express consent for the call to be made or has an established business relationship with the caller shall not be considered an abandoned call if the message begins within two (2) seconds of the called person's completed greeting.

(ii) Calls made by or on behalf of tax-exempt nonprofit organizations are not covered by paragraph (a)(6) of this section.

(7) Use any technology to dial any telephone number for the purpose of determining whether the line is a facsimile or voice line.

(b) All artificial or prerecorded telephone messages shall:

(1) At the beginning of the message, state clearly the identity of the business, individual, or other entity that is responsible for initiating the call. If a business is responsible for initiating the call, the name under which the entity is registered to conduct business with the State Corporation Commission (or comparable regulatory authority) must be stated, and

(2) During or after the message, state clearly the telephone number (other than that of the autodialer or prerecorded message player that placed the call) of such business, other entity, or individual. The telephone number provided may not be a 900 number or any other number for which charges exceed local or long distance transmission charges. For telemarketing messages to residential telephone subscribers, such telephone number must permit any individual to make a Do-Not-Call request during regular business hours for the duration of the telemarketing campaign.

(c) No person or entity shall initiate any telephone solicitation, as defined in paragraph (f)(9) of this section, to:

(1) Any residential telephone subscriber before the hour of 8 a.m. or after 9 p.m. (local time at the called party's location), or

(2) A residential telephone subscriber who has registered his or her telephone number on the national do-not-call registry of persons who do not wish to receive telephone solicitations that is maintained by the federal government. Such Do-Not-Call registrations must be honored for a period of 5 years. Any

person or entity making telephone solicitations (or on whose behalf telephone solicitations are made) will not be liable for violating this requirement if:

(i) It can demonstrate that the violation is the result of error and that as part of its routine business practice, it meets the following standards:

(A) Written procedures. It has established and implemented written procedures to comply with the national Do-Not-Call rules;

(B) Training of personnel. It has trained its personnel, and any entity assisting in its compliance, in procedures established pursuant to the national do-not-call rules;

(C) Recording. It has maintained and recorded a list of telephone numbers that the seller may not contact;

(D) Accessing the national do-not-call database. It uses a process to prevent telephone solicitations to any telephone number on any list established pursuant to the Do-Not-Call rules, employing a version of the national Do-Not-Call Registry obtained from the administrator of the registry no more than three months prior to the date any call is made, and maintains records documenting this process; and

(E) Purchasing the national Do-Not-Call database. It uses a process to ensure that it does not sell, rent, lease, purchase or use the national Do-Not-Call database, or any part thereof, for any purpose except compliance with this section and any such state or federal law to prevent telephone solicitations to telephone numbers registered on the ational database. It purchases access to the relevant Do-Not-Call data from the administrator of the national database and does not participate in any arrangement to share the cost of accessing the national database, including any arrangement with telemarketers who may not divide the costs to access the national database among various client sellers; or

(ii) It has obtained the subscriber's prior express invitation or permission. Such permission must be evidenced by a signed, written agreement between the consumer and seller which states that the consumer agrees to be contacted by this seller and includes the telephone number to which the calls may be placed; or

(iii) The telemarketer making the call has a personal relationship with the recipient of the call.

(d) No person or entity shall initiate any call for telemarketing purposes to a residential telephone subscriber unless such person or entity has instituted procedures for maintaining a list of persons who request not to receive telemarketing calls made by or on behalf of that person or entity. The procedures instituted must meet the following minimum standards:

(1) Written policy. Persons or entities making calls for telemarketing purposes must have a written policy, available upon demand, for maintaining a Do-Not-Call List.

(2) Training of personnel engaged in telemarketing. Personnel engaged in any aspect of telemarketing must be informed and trained in the existence and use of the Do-Not-Call List.

(3) Recording, disclosure of do-not-call requests. If a person or entity making a call for telemarketing purposes (or on whose behalf such a call is made) receives a request from a residential telephone subscriber not to receive calls from that person or entity, the person or entity must record the request and place the subscriber's name, if provided, and telephone number on the Do-Not-Call List at the time the request is made. Persons or entities making calls for telemarketing purposes (or on whose behalf such calls are made) must honor a residential subscriber's do-not-call request within a reasonable time from the date such request is made. This period may not exceed thirty days from the date of such request. If such requests are recorded or maintained by a party other than the person or entity on whose behalf the telemarketing call is made, the person or entity on whose behalf the telemarketing call is made will be liable for any failures to honor the Do-Not-Call request. A person or entity making a call for telemarketing purposes must obtain a consumer's prior express permission to share or forward the consumer's request not to be called to a party other than the person or entity on whose behalf a telemarketing call is made or an affiliated entity.

(4) Identification of sellers and telemarketers. A person or entity making a call for telemarketing purposes must provide the called party with the name of the individual caller, the name of the person or entity on whose behalf the call is being made, and a telephone number or address at which the person or entity may be contacted. The telephone number provided may not be a 900 number or any other number for which charges exceed local or long distance transmission charges.

(5) Affiliated persons or entities. In the absence of a specific request by the subscriber to the contrary, a residential subscriber's Do-Not-Call request shall apply to the particular business entity making the call (or on whose behalf a call is made), and will not apply to affiliated entities unless the consumer reasonably would expect them to be included given the identification of the caller and the product being advertised.

(6) Maintenance of do-not-call lists. A person or entity making calls for tele-

marketing purposes must maintain a record of a caller's request not to receive further telemarketing calls. A Do-Not-Call request must be honored for 5 years from the time the request is made.

(7) Tax-exempt nonprofit organizations are not required to comply with 64.1200(d).

(e) The rules set forth in paragraph (c) and (d) of this section are applicable to any person or entity making telephone solicitations or telemarketing calls to wireless telephone numbers to the extent described in the Commission's Report and Order, CG Docket No. 02-278, FCC 03-153, ``Rules and Regulations Implementing the Telephone Consumer Protection Act of 1991.''

(f) As used in this section:

(1) The terms automatic telephone dialing system and autodialer mean equipment which has the capacity to store or produce telephone numbers to be called using a random or sequential number generator and to dial such numbers.

(2) The term emergency purposes means calls made necessary in any situation affecting the health and safety of consumers.

(3) The term established business relationship means a prior or existing relationship formed by a voluntary two-way communication between a person or entity and a residential subscriber with or without an exchange of consideration, on the basis of the subscriber's purchase or transaction with the entity within the eighteen (18) months immediately preceding the date of the telephone call or on the basis of the subscriber's inquiry or application regarding products or services offered by the entity within the three months immediately preceding the date of the call, which relationship has not been previously terminated by either party.

(i) The subscriber's seller-specific Do-Not-Call request, as set forth in paragraph (d)(3) of this section, terminates an established business relationship for purposes of telemarketing and telephone solicitation even if the subscriber continues to do business with the seller.

(ii) The subscriber's established business relationship with a particular business entity does not extend to affiliated entities unless the subscriber would reasonably expect them to be included given the nature and type of goods or services offered by the affiliate and the identity of the affiliate.

[Note to paragraph(f)(3): Paragraph 64.1200(f)(3) is stayed as of October 14, 2003, as it applies to the time limitations on facsimile advertisements. The Federal Communications Commission will publish a document in the Federal Register when the stay is lifted.]

(4) The term facsimile broadcaster means a person or entity that transmits messages to telephone facsimile machines on behalf of another person or entity for a fee.

(5) The term seller means the person or entity on whose behalf a telephone call or message is initiated for the purpose of encouraging the purchase or rental of, or investment in, property, goods, or services, which is transmitted to any person.

(6) The term telemarketer means the person or entity that initiates a telephone call or message for the purpose of encouraging the purchase or rental of, or investment in, property, goods, or services, which is transmitted to any person.

(7) The term telemarketing means the initiation of a telephone call or message for the purpose of encouraging the purchase or rental of, or investment in, property, goods, or services, which is transmitted to any person.

(8) The term telephone facsimile machine means equipment which has the capacity to transcribe text or images, or both, from paper into an electronic signal and to transmit that signal over a regular telephone line, or to transcribe text or images (or both) from an electronic signal received over a regular telephone line onto paper.

(9) The term telephone solicitation means the initiation of a telephone call or message for the purpose of encouraging the purchase or rental of, or investment in, property, goods, or services, which is transmitted to any person, but such term does not include a call or message:

(i) To any person with that person's prior express invitation or permission;

(ii) To any person with whom the caller has an established business relationship; or

(iii) By or on behalf of a tax-exempt nonprofit organization.

(10) The term unsolicited advertisement means any material advertising the commercial availability or quality of any property, goods, or services which is transmitted to any person without that person's prior express invitation or permission.

(11) The term personal relationship means any family member, friend, or acquaintance of the telemarketer making the call.

(g) Beginning January 1, 2004, common carriers shall:

(1) When providing local exchange service, provide an annual notice, via an insert in the subscriber's bill, of the right to give or revoke a notification of an objection to receiving telephone solicitations pursuant to the national do-not-call database maintained by the federal government and the methods by

which such rights may be exercised by the subscriber. The notice must be clear and conspicuous and include, at a minimum, the Internet address and toll-free number that residential telephone subscribers may use to register on the national database.

(2) When providing service to any person or entity for the purpose of making telephone solicitations, make a one-time notification to such person or entity of the national Do-Not-Call requirements, including, at a minimum, citation to 47 CFR 64.1200 and 16 CFR 310. Failure to receive such notification will not serve as a defense to any person or entity making telephone solicitations from violations of this section.

(h) The administrator of the national do-not-call registry that is maintained by the federal government shall make the telephone numbers in the database available to the States so that a State may use the telephone numbers that relate to such State as part of any database, list or listing system maintained by such State for the regulation of telephone solicitations.

How To Sue
A Telemarketer

Notes

ADDENDUM 3

Law Offices of Stephen I. Ostrow

2533 South Highway 101, Suite 280, Cardiff by the Sea, CA 92007
(760) 944-0066, fax (760) 944-0067
steveostrow@gmail.com

September 26, 2007

Att: PRESIDENT OF XXXXXXXXXXXXXXXXXXXXX
XXXXXXXXXXXXXXXXXXXX
Deerfield Beach, Florida 33441

Re: 10 DAY NOTICE OF SUIT- VIOLATION OF TELEPHONE
CONSUMER PROTECTION ACT

Dear XXXXXXXXXXXXXXXXX

I represent myself, in pro per, who was solicited by or on behalf of your company, without my permission, at home, notwithstanding the home telephone number was registered with the National Do-Not-Call Registry at least 30 days prior to the un-welcomed and uninvited solicitation. You telephoned the home number 858-793-0633 on September 25, 2007 at approximately 2:30 pm seeking to sell your unrequested loan services.

This letter is to provide you with formal notice of my intension to sue under the Federal Telephone Consumer Protection Act 47 U.S.C. 227 and the FCC regulations promulgated under the statute. This statute and regulations prohibit "cold call" tele-phone solicitations without prior express permission after registering with the National Do Not Call Registry. The statute and regulations provide for a minimum $500.00 (FIVE HUNDRED DOLLARS) statutory recovery for each violation if the above provision or regulations are violated. My client has calculated 1 violation(s) of the statute. If it is determined that these violations(s) were willful or knowing as defined in the Telecommunication Act, the recovery would be tripled for each violation. Let me assure you, it is impossible for the solicitation to occur randomly since you called the homeowner by name.

Thus, the 1 unsolicited telemarketing call is/are subject to treble damages and court costs.

RECYCLED PAPER

You are further given notice that to the extent you are in possession and/or control documents or other evidence relevant to this matter, you are under a continuing legal duty to secure such documents or evidence from loss, altercation, or destruction. Failure to do so may result in sanctions, forfeiture of legal rights, and a separate action for spoliation of evidence.

I am willing to settle this matter for $500 (FIVE HUNDRED DOLLARS) if a cashier's check for the above amount is received within ten (10) days of the date of this letter. If for any reason you feel you have not violated the TCPA please contact me in writing with those reasons. If settlement is not possible please inform me so that suit can be initiated. Suit would be for the statutory imposed treble damages of $1500.00 (ONE THOUSAND FIVE HUNDRED) plus court costs. If you would like to discuss this matter, please feel free to call me at my office.

GOVERN YOURSELF ACCORDINGLY.

Very truly yours,

Stephen Ostrow

RECYCLED PAPER

ADDENDUM 4

<table>
<tr><td>**SC-100**</td><td>**Plaintiff's Claim and ORDER to Go to Small Claims Court**</td><td>*Clerk stamps date here when form is filed.*</td></tr>
</table>

Notice to the person being sued:

- You are the Defendant if your name is listed in ② on page 2 of this form. The person suing you is the Plaintiff, listed in ① on page 2.
- You and the Plaintiff must go to court on the trial date listed below. If you do not go to court, you may lose the case.
- If you lose, the court can order that your wages, money, or property be taken to pay this claim.
- Bring witnesses, receipts, and any evidence you need to prove your case.
- Read this form and all pages attached to understand the claim against you and to protect your rights.

Aviso al Demandado:

- Usted es el Demandado si su nombre figura en ② de la página 2 de este formulario. La persona que lo demanda es el Demandante, la que figura en ① de la página 2.
- Usted y el Demandante tienen que presentarse en la corte en la fecha del juicio indicada a continuación. Si no se presenta, puede perder el caso.
- Si pierde el caso la corte podría ordenar que le quiten de su sueldo, dinero u otros bienes para pagar este reclamo.
- Lleve testigos, recibos y cualquier otra prueba que necesite para probar su caso.
- Lea este formulario y todas las páginas adjuntas para entender la demanda en su contra y para proteger sus derechos.

Fill in court name and street address:
Superior Court of California, County of
San Diego, North County Division
325 S. Melrose Ave,
Vista, CA 92081

Clerk fills in case number and case name:
Case Number:
123456789
Case Name:
PLAINTIFF v. DEFENDANT

Order to Go to Court

The people in ① and ② must go to court: *(Clerk fills out section below.)*

Trial Date	→	Date	Time	Department	Name and address of court if different from above
	1.				
	2.				
	3.				

Date: _____ Clerk, by _____, Deputy

Instructions for the person suing:

- You are the Plaintiff. The person you are suing is the Defendant.
- *Before* you fill out this form, read Form SC-150, *Information for the Plaintiff (Small Claims),* to know your rights. Get SC-150 at any courthouse or county law library, or go to: *www.courtinfo.ca.gov/forms*
- Fill out pages 2 and 3 of this form. Then make copies of **all** pages of this form. (Make 1 copy for each party named in this case and an extra copy for yourself.) Take or mail the original and these copies to the court clerk's office and pay the filing fee. The clerk will write the date of your trial in the box above.
- You must have someone at least 18—not you or anyone else listed in this case—give each Defendant a court-stamped copy of all 5 pages of this form and any pages this form tells you to attach. There are special rules for "serving," or delivering, this form to public entities, associations, and some businesses. See Forms SC-104, SC-104B, and SC-104C
- **Go to court on your trial date listed above.** Bring witnesses, receipts, and any evidence you need to prove your case.

Judicial Council of California, www.courtinfo.ca.gov
Revised January 1, 2006, Mandatory Form
Code of Civil Procedure, §§ 116.110 et seq.,
116.220(c), 116.340(g)

Plaintiff's Claim and ORDER to Go to Small Claims Court (Small Claims)

SC-100, Page 1 of 5
→

American LegalNet, Inc.
www.FormsWorkflow.com

124

Plaintiff *(list names):* _____

(1) **The Plaintiff (the person, business, or public entity that is suing) is:**

Name: _____YOU_____ Phone: ( )

Street address: _your address_ _____
Street   City   State   Zip

Mailing address *(if different):* _____
Street   City   State   Zip

If more than one Plaintiff, list next Plaintiff here:

Name: _____ Phone: ( )

Street address: _____
Street   City   State   Zip

Mailing address *(if different):* _____
Street   City   State   Zip

☐ *Check here if more than 2 Plaintiffs and attach Form SC-100A.*

☐ *Check here if either Plaintiff listed above is doing business under a fictitious name. If so, attach Form SC-103.*

(2) **The Defendant (the person, business, or public entity being sued) is:**

Name: The A-hole telemarketer***careful about the dba and correct business   Phone: ( )

Street address: _____address of business_____
Street   City   State   Zip

Mailing address *(if different):* _____
Street   City   State   Zip

If more than one Defendant, list next Defendant here:

Name: _____ Phone: ( )

Street address: _____
Street   City   State   Zip

Mailing address *(if different):* _____
Street   City   State   Zip

☐ *Check here if more than 2 Defendants and attach Form SC-100A.*

☐ *Check here if any Defendant is on active military duty, and write his or her name here:* _____

(3) **The Plaintiff claims the Defendant owes $** 1500 **.** *(Explain below):*

a. Why does the Defendant owe the Plaintiff money? e.g. Without permission or a prior business relationship, Defendant faxed an unsolicited advertisement to me in violation of the Telephone Consumer Protection Act 47 U.S.C. 227

b. When did this happen? *(Date):* 10/10/2010

If no specific date, give the time period: *Date started:* _____ *Through:* _____

c. How did you calculate the money owed to you? *(Do not include court costs or fees for service.)* _____
Statutory fees for violation

☐ *Check here if you need more space. Attach one sheet of paper or Form MC-031 and write "SC-100, Item 3" at the top.*

---

(4) **You must ask the Defendant (in person, in writing, or by phone) to pay you before you sue. Have you done this?** ☑ Yes ☐ No
If no, explain why not: _____

(5) **Why are you filing your claim at this courthouse?**
This courthouse covers the area *(check the one that applies):*

a. ☑ (1) Where the Defendant lives or does business.   (4) Where a contract (written or spoken) was made,
    (2) Where the Plaintiff's property was damaged.   signed, performed, or broken by the Defendant *or*
    (3) Where the Plaintiff was injured.   where the Defendant lived or did business when
    the Defendant made the contract.

b. ☐ Where the buyer or lessee signed the contract lives now, or lived when the contract was made, if this claim is about an offer or contract for personal, family, or household goods, services, or loans. *(Code Civ. Proc., § 395(b).)*

c. ☐ Where the buyer signed the contract, lives now, or lived when the contract was made, if this claim is about a retail installment contract (like a credit card). *(Civil Code, § 1812.10.)*

d. ☐ Where the buyer signed the contract, lives now, or lived when the contract was made, or where the vehicle is permanently garaged, if this claim is about a vehicle finance sale. *(Civil Code, § 2984.4.)*

e. ☐ Other *(specify):* _____

(6) **List the zip code of the place checked in ⑤ above** *(if you know):* 92007

(7) **Is your claim about an attorney-client fee dispute?** ☐ Yes ☑ No
If yes, and if you have had arbitration, fill out Form SC-101, attach it to this form, and check here: ☐

(8) **Are you suing a public entity?** ☐ Yes ☑ No
If yes, you must file a written claim with the entity first. ☐ A claim was filed on *(date):* _____
If the public entity denies your claim or does not answer within the time allowed by law, you can file this form.

(9) **Have you filed more than 12 other small claims within the last 12 months in California?**
☐ Yes ☑ No   *If yes, the filing fee for this case will be higher.*

(10) **I understand that by filing a claim in small claims court, I have no right to appeal this claim.**

(11) I have not filed, and understand that I cannot file, more than two small claims cases for more than $2,500 in California during this calendar year.

I declare, under penalty of perjury under California State law, that the information above and on any attachments to this form is true and correct.

Date: _____   YOU _____   ▶ _____
    Plaintiff types or prints name here   *Plaintiff signs here*

Date: _____   _____   ▶ _____
    Second Plaintiff types or prints name here   *Second Plaintiff signs here*

Requests for Accommodations
Assistive listening systems, computer-assisted, real-time captioning, or sign language interpreter services are available if you ask at least 5 days before the trial. Contact the clerk's office for Form MC-410, *Request for Accommodations by Persons With Disabilities and Response. (Civil Code, § 54.8.)*

126

How To Sue
A Telemarketer

Notes

ADDENDUM 5

Name and Address of Court:

PLAINTIFF/DEMANDANTE (Name, address, and telephone number of each):	SMALL CLAIMS CASE NO. 123456789
YOU	DEFENDANT/DEMANDADO (Name, address, and telephone number of each):
	The A-hole telemarketer

Telephone No.:

Telephone No.:

Telephone No.:

Telephone No.:

☐ See attached sheet for additional plaintiffs and defendants.

SMALL CLAIMS SUBPOENA
FOR PERSONAL APPEARANCE AND PRODUCTION OF DOCUMENTS
AND THINGS AT TRIAL OR HEARING AND DECLARATION

THE PEOPLE OF THE STATE OF CALIFORNIA, TO *(name, address, and telephone number of witness, if known)*:

1. **YOU ARE ORDERED TO APPEAR AS A WITNESS** in this case at the date, time, and place shown in the box below UNLESS your appearance is excused as indicated in box 4b below or you make an agreement with the person named in item 2 below.

   a. Date: same as trial date Time: ☐ Dept.: ☐ Div.: ☐ Room:
   b. Address: court house address

2. **IF YOU HAVE ANY QUESTIONS ABOUT THE TIME OR DATE YOU ARE TO APPEAR, OR IF YOU WANT TO BE CERTAIN THAT YOUR PRESENCE IS REQUIRED, CONTACT THE FOLLOWING PERSON BEFORE THE DATE ON WHICH YOU ARE TO APPEAR:**

   a. Name of subpoenaing party: YOU b. Telephone number: your phone no.

3. **Witness Fees:** You are entitled to witness fees and mileage actually traveled both ways, as provided by law, if you request them at the time of service. You may request them before your scheduled appearance from the person named in item 2.

PRODUCTION OF DOCUMENTS AND THINGS
(Complete item 4 only if you want the witness to produce documents and things at the trial or hearing.)

4. YOU ARE *(item a or b must be checked)*:

   a. ☐ Ordered to appear in person and to produce the records described in the declaration on page two. The personal attendance of the custodian or other qualified witness and the production of the original records are required by this subpoena. The procedure authorized by Evidence Code sections 1560(b), 1561, and 1562 will not be deemed sufficient compliance with this subpoena.

   b. ☐ Not required to appear in person if you produce (i) the records described in the declaration on page two and (ii) a completed declaration of custodian of records in compliance with Evidence Code sections 1560, 1561, 1562, and 1271. (1) Place a copy of the records in an envelope (or other wrapper). Enclose the original declaration of the custodian with the records. Seal the envelope. (2) Attach a copy of this subpoena to the envelope or write on the envelope the case name and number; your name; and the date, time, and place from item 1 in the box above. (3) Place this first envelope in an outer envelope, seal it, and mail it to the clerk of the court at the address in item 1. (4) Mail a copy of your declaration to the attorney or party listed at the top of this form.

5. **IF YOU HAVE BEEN SERVED WITH THIS SUBPOENA AS A CUSTODIAN OF CONSUMER OR EMPLOYEE RECORDS UNDER CODE OF CIVIL PROCEDURE SECTION 1985.3 OR 1985.6 AND A MOTION TO QUASH OR AN OBJECTION HAS BEEN SERVED ON YOU, A COURT ORDER OR AGREEMENT OF THE PARTIES, WITNESSES, *AND* CONSUMER OR EMPLOYEE AFFECTED MUST BE OBTAINED BEFORE YOU ARE REQUIRED TO PRODUCE CONSUMER OR EMPLOYEE RECORDS.**

> **DISOBEDIENCE OF THIS SUBPOENA MAY BE PUNISHED AS CONTEMPT BY THIS COURT. YOU WILL ALSO BE LIABLE FOR THE SUM OF FIVE HUNDRED DOLLARS AND ALL DAMAGES RESULTING FROM YOUR FAILURE TO OBEY.**

[SEAL] Date issued:

Clerk, by _____ , Deputy

(See reverse for declaration in support of subpoena) Page one of three

Form Adopted for Mandatory Use Judicial Council of California SC-107 [Rev. January 1, 2000]	**SMALL CLAIMS SUBPOENA AND DECLARATION**	Code of Civil Procedure, § 1985 et seq. American LegalNet, Inc. [www.USCourtForms.com]

PLAINTIFF/PETITIONER: YOU	CASE NUMBER:
DEFENDANT/RESPONDENT: A-hole telemarketer	123456789

DECLARATION IN SUPPORT OF
SMALL CLAIMS SUBPOENA FOR PERSONAL APPEARANCE
AND PRODUCTION OF DOCUMENT AND THINGS AT TRIAL OR HEARING
(Code Civil Procedure sections 1985, 1987.5)

1. I, the undersigned, declare I am the ☑ plaintiff ☐ defendant ☐ judgment creditor
   ☐ other *(specify)*: in the above entitled action.

2. The witness has possession or control of the following documents or other things and shall produce them at the time and place specified on the *Small Claims Subpoena* on the first page of this form.

   a. ☑ For trial or hearing *(specify the exact documents or other things to be produced by the witness)*:
   > See attachment 2a

   ☑ Continued on Attachment 2a.
   b. ☐ After trial to enforce a judgment *(specify the exact documents or other things to be produced by the party who is the judgment debtor or other witness possessing records relating to the judgment debtor)*:

   (1) ☐ Payroll receipts, stubs, and other records concerning employment of the party. Receipts, invoices, documents, and other papers or records concerning any and all accounts receivable of the party.

   (2) ☐ Bank account statements, canceled checks, and check registers from any and all bank accounts in which the party has an interest.

   (3) ☐ Savings account passbooks and statements, savings and loan account passbooks and statements, and credit union share account passbooks and statements of the party.

   (4) ☐ Stock certificates, bonds, money market certificates, and any other records, documents, or papers concerning all investments of the party.

   (5) ☐ California registration certificates and ownership certificates for all vehicles registered to the party.

   (6) ☐ Deeds to any and all real property owned or being purchased by the party.

   (7) ☐ Other *(specify)*:

3. Good cause exists for the production of the documents or other things described in paragraph 2 for the following reasons:
   e.g. Prohibition on the use of artificial or prerecorded voice telemarketing, 47 U.S.C. 227(b)(1)(B). Failure to supply a written do not call policy, Title 47, CFR 64.1601, 64.1200(d)(1). Failure to identify caller address or telephone, Title 47, CFR 64.1200(b)(1) & (2). Failure to comply with Telemarketing Sales Rule of keeping records, 16 CFR 310.5

   ☐ Continued on Attachment 3.

4. These documents are material to the issues involved in this case for the following reasons:
   e.g. Defendant used automated telemarketing equipment to transmit multiple banned prerecorded advertisements to residential phone lines without written permission from Plaintiff in violation. Also, Plaintiff's number on national do not call lists and to prove call violation of the Code. Also, to show Defendant did not have a Do Not Call Policy or maintain telemarketing records as required by code.

   ☐ Continued on Attachment 4.

I declare under penalty of perjury under the laws of the State of California that the foregoing is true and correct.

Date:

..........YOU.......... ▶
(TYPE OR PRINT NAME) (SIGNATURE OF PARTY)

(See proof of service on page three)

SC-107 [Rev. January 1, 2000]	**SMALL CLAIMS SUBPOENA AND DECLARATION**	Page two of three

129

Attachment to Supbena Form _____ Plaintiff v. Defendant,
Case No. 123456789)

All of the following under the defendant's possession, custody or control:

1. All defendant's telemarketing scripts and telephone promotional materials.

2. Defendant's telemarketing contracts with phone carriers and 3rd parties in effect from _____ though _____ (the period of contact with plaintiff).

3. Defendant's documents, electronic info, records and recordings of all pre-recorded phone scripts and telemarketing materials in use from _____ though _____ (the period of contact with plaintiff).

4. All third party telemarketing records with the defendant from _____ though _____ (the period of contact with plaintiff).

5. The defendant's telemarketing phone bill from _____ though _____ (the period of contact with plaintiff).

6. Defendant's purchase receipts of automated telemarketing equipment used from _____ though _____ (the period of contact with plaintiff).

7. Defendant's copy of the application to the telephone corporation to send out automatic telemarketing announcements from _____ though _____ (the period of contact with plaintiff).

8. Defendant's copy of the approval of application from the telephone corporation to send out automatic telemarketing announcements from _____ though _____ (the period of contact with plaintiff).

9. Defendant's procedures to handle telemarketing do not call requests from _____ though _____ (the period of contact with plaintiff).

10. Complaints and demand letters received by defendant related to their automated telemarketing efforts.

11. Defendant's telemarketing training manual used from _____ though _____ (the period of contact with plaintiff).

12. Defendant's bank statements and checks paid for the telemarketing budget from _____ though _____ (the period of contact with plaintiff).

13. Defendant's memos, emails, notes, internal documents reflecting telemarketing budget from _____ though _____ (the period of contact with plaintiff)

130

TRIAL BRIEF

Plaintiff submits the following trial brief in support of its complaint:

1. Unsolicited Advertisement

The term "unsolicited advertisement" is defined by the law as "any material advertising the commercial availability or quality of any property, goods, or services which is transmitted to any person without that person's prior express invitation or permission, in writing or otherwise." Offers for free goods or services that are part of an overall marketing campaign to sell property, goods, or services constitute "advertising the commercial availability or quality of any property, goods, or services."

AUTHORITY: 47 U.S.C. § 227(a)(5); Report and Order, 18 FCC Rcd 14014 at 140 (2003).

2. Liability- Calls made "on behalf of" a party

The Telephone Consumer Protection Act reaches not only the entity making the telephone solicitation, but also any entity "on whose behalf" such calls are made. If you determine that the calls were made "on behalf of" the defendant, then the defendant is responsible for violations of the Telephone Consumer Protection Act from such calls.

AUTHORITY: Worsham v. Nationwide Ins. Co., 138 Md.App. 487, 772 A.2d 868 (Md.App. 2001). 365 Md. 268, 778 A.2d 383 (Md. 2001); Chair King, Inc., v. GTE Mobilnet of Houston, Inc., 135 S.W.3d 365 (Tex. App. 2004); Hooters of Augusta, Inc. v.

Nicholson, 245 Ga.App. 363, 537 S.E.2d 468 (Ga.App. 2000) reco'n den'd (Jul. 27, 2000);

3. Agency- Ratification

A person can be held responsible for the acts of a third party if the person "ratifies" the acts of that third party. Ratification exists if the person becomes aware of what the third party did and with that knowledge either retains the benefits of the third party's acts or fails to repudiate those acts promptly upon learning of them. If you find that the defendant ratified the actions of the marketing company, then the defendant is responsible for violations of the Telephone Consumer Protection Act from the actions that marketing company caused.

AUTHORITY: Restatement (Second) of Agency, §§ 82, 94, 98-99]. Hunter v. Hyder, 236 S.C. 378, 114 S.E.2d 493 (S.C. 1960) (retaining the benefit) "But even if Stack was an independent contractor, and the defendant did not participate in the trespass, the defendant under the facts here appearing, would, nevertheless, be liable for the value of the timber as property of the plaintiff of which it has had the benefit." Citing Abbott v. Sumter Lumber Co., 93 S.C. 131, 76 S.E. 146 (S.C. 1912).

a) Direct Participation

"A director, officer, or agent is not liable for torts of the corporation or of other officers or agents merely because of his office. He is liable for torts in which he has participated or which he has authorized or directed."

AUTHORITY: 19 C.J.S. Corporations § 845; cited in BPS, Inc. v. Worthy, 362 S.C. 319, 608 S.E.2d 155 (S.C.App.,2005); 19

Am.Jur.2d Corporations, 4, Liability for Torts: § 1382, cited in Hunt v. Rabon, 275 S.C. 475, 272 S.E.2d 643 (S.C., 1980).

b) Lack of Proper Supervision

A director, officer, or agent of a corporation can be held responsible for acts of subordinates where such a person could, in the exercise of ordinary and reasonable supervision, have detected the wrongdoing of such subordinate.

AUTHORITY: BPS, Inc. v. Worthy, 362 S.C. 319, 608 S.E.2d 155 (S.C.App.,2005); 19 Am.Jur.2d Corporations, 4, Liability for Torts: § 1382 (cited in Hunt v. Rabon, 275 S.C. 475, 272 S.E.2d 643 (S.C., 1980)).

4. Actual Damages Irrelevant

It is not necessary that you find the plaintiff has any actual injury or actual damages.

AUTHORITY: Purtle v. Eldridge Auto Sales, Inc., 91 F.3d 797 (6th Cir. 1996). ("There is no requirement that [plaintiff] suffer actual damages to recover under the TILA."); BMG Music v. Gonzalez, 430 F.3d 888 (7th Cir, 2005) (No jury question when mandatory statutory damages sought in lieu of actual damages under Copyright Act.); Scofield v. Telecable of Overland Park, Inc., 751 F.Supp. 1499, 1521 (D.Kan.1990) (When the statute provides for liquidated statutory damages, "the court must award liquidated damages at a minimum, even in the absence of actual damages.")

How To Sue
A Telemarketer

**Metaphysical Exercise
to Overcome Telemarketer Hatred**

1. I hate all telemarketers

2. I hate some telemarketers

3. I look for the good in everyone

4. There is some good in everyone

5. Telemarketers serve some public good

6. Some mummies and puppies
   love telemarketers

7. Some telemarketers love their
   mummies and puppies

8. I am creating new experiences for
   myself and others

9. I am creating a better world for
   myself and others

10. I no longer hate telemarketers,
    I just dislike them!

EPILOGUE

The year was 1789 and new America just kicked England's ass to gain its independence. The founding fathers and generals gathered between New York and Boston preparing for the legendary Constitution. Washington D.C. was not even a blip on the map. Most of the focus was deliberating on the past abuses perpetrated by the Crown against the Colonialists. Mail was delivered by horseback, and no one received junk mail or unwelcome knocks on their door. Homes were so spread out that the community bulletin boards announced markets, bargains, and commercials. The train remained 50 years away, and the invention of the telephone 100 years. Consumers came to the message. The hot topic at the convention: freedom of speech.

Should speech be censored in any way? Some founding fathers, knowing that there was always a pain-in-the-ass element in society, begged for some "reasonable restraint language" for the general good. Finally it was decided that the language be pure, and the Bill of Rights encapsulated the First Amendment of Freedom of Speech. It was also agreed that if any jerk abused that privilege, a musket shot or public dunking would be appropriate (off the record).

Obviously much has changed since the ink on the First Amendment dried. The balancing act between commercialism and privacy continues on. Some devout Americans believe that not to consume is unpatriotic, and that it is the telemarketer's patriotic duty to bring his products into the consumer's face. Dan Aykroyd would respond, "Jane, you ignorant slut!"

"No Solicitors" signs have appeared on residence and office doors. It's not that we have become anti-social, but rather desire to control the time and place we want to hear your bullshit on why we need your product. These signs have no value unless there is a corresponding "no trespassing" law in the code books.

Congress has responded with the TCPA and a national Do-Not-Call Registry. The scales have tipped in favor of personal privacy over commercial greed; however, the telemarketers aren't rolling over easily. What will it take to put these scumbags out of business? Crime is not eliminated, but controlled. Telemarketers will find a devious way to stick around. It's now a joint effort between government and community to control its parasites. Laws are passed, and attorney generals take moderate action. But in this world of limited budgets, it is the consuming public who will control the thermostat on telemarketing harassment.

Telemarketing busting is growing. The use of the Small Claims and Superior Courts to fight back is making a difference to the telemarketing industry. The *cost of doing business* is escalating by these court judgments which are increasing daily. Yes, people are collecting against the telemarketers. Judges and Commissioners are becoming more and more familiar with the TCPA and the public's ability to collect judgments thereunder. Companies think twice, sometimes three times, before employing the cold calling callous commercial cranks.

Judgments can start at a simple $500 for any one telemarketing violation; sometimes trebled to $1500 for intentional acts or for "deceit upon the court". Telemarketing companies and their associates get hit harder their second, third, and multiple appearances. Multiple violations are being stacked together making the trip to the courthouse worthwhile. Companies must consider a possible adverse judgment when deciding whether to go the telemarketer route, and judgments become thorns in their sides when calculating their potential profits for violation of this "petty illegality". Yes, we can make a difference; yes, we can affect the way others do business.

Another patriotic theory is that it is your duty to prosecute these bastards into submission. The 1960's Civil Rights movement made its impact through the courts. Woman's Rights of Privacy made its impact through the Courts. As more and more people take action, the awareness of the public's fundamental right of privacy and peace in the home is heightened. **YES WE CAN!** We not only deserve to have our homes free from telemarketers unwanted disturbances, it is our constitutional, legislative, and common law right to choose whom we allow into our homes. And that includes these telemarketers. And so it is.

About Steve Ostrow

Migrating from the trains of Brooklyn, to the snows of SUNY Buffalo, to the mellow waves of Southern California, Steve graduated Pepperdine University School of Law in 1979. The courtroom was a natural setting for an east-coast wise guy, combining his wit and principles to create a non-traditional law practice by-the-sea.

Contributing to a non-conforming legal lifestyle, Steve has studied yoga and meditation, acting and improvisation, and has travelled with the Grateful Dead. Combining a unique view-point to the arduous areas of the law, Steve has sat as a small claims judge in Los Angeles and San Diego Counties as well. With an office on the beach in Cardiff-by-the-Sea, he manages to blend the Southern California lifestyle of both acting and practicing law into the California dream with his fashionable collection of aloha wear.

Steve lives in Solana Beach, California, with "Amigo", the world's worst watchdog, but most unconditionally loving companion. Taking advantage of the opportunity to travel the world and experience multi-cultures, he enjoys the simple pleasures of hiking the beach and canyons around San Diego, as well as a good game of tennis and ping pong.

Looking back at the highs and lows over the last 30 years as a concerned citizen and lawyer, Steve sums it up with a quote from one of his favorite poets, "What a long, strange trip it has been!"

About Ozmo Kramer

In 1996, Michael Richards played a lawyer in the movie Trial and Error. Keeping the playing field fair, the celebrity impersonation of Ozmo Kramer came alive shortly thereafter. After doing 20 years of stand-up routine before courtrooms across California, Ozmo Kramer was launched Halloween 1996 at a Halloween festival in Encinitas, California. If Kramer could play a lawyer, a lawyer could play Kramer. Why not? Wanting to give up his day job and polyester ties, Ozmo started appearing at numerous corporate and entertainment venues.

A graduate of Rick Stevens School of Improvisation in San Diego, and a well seasoned Toastmaster, spontaneous success was achieved in the look-alike and improvisational worlds. In his first year of improvisational comedy, Ozmo was presented with the prestigious Reel Award for Big Mouth Comedy by the International Celebrity Images and his look-alike peers. As the Seinfeld series wound down, Ozmo won numerous Seinfeld look-alike type events. Since its last episode, Ozmo has filled the gap for Seinfeld fans who have demanded more than re-runs.

Since the creation of Ozmo, appearances have been made around the globe. Television appearances include the Tonight Show, Jimmy Kimmel and Ellen Degeneres Show, as well as television specials.

For more information, please visit **www.ozmokramer.com**.

Breinigsville, PA USA
07 April 2010
235637BV00001B/2/P